THE
HEALINGS OF CHRIST

THE HEALINGS OF CHRIST

Paul Sédir

FRIENDS
IN SPIRIT

First published in French as
Les Guérisons du Christ
A.-L. Legrand, Éditeur
Sotteville-lez-Rouen, 1926
First English edition © Friends in Spirit, 2024
an imprint of Sophia Perennis
Translation © Friends in Spirit 2024
Series Editor: James R. Wetmore

All rights reserved

No part of this book may be reproduced or transmitted,
in any form or by any means, without permission

For information, address:
Friends in Spirit
Box 931, Philmont, NY 12565

ISBN 978-1-59731-227-1 (pbk)
ISBN 978-1-59731-200-4 (cloth)

Cover Design: Michael Schrauzer

CONTENTS

Biographical Sketch i
Introduction 1

CHAPTER I
Mystical Healings 23

Gospel Quotes 25
The Mystical Healer 29
Necessary Precautions 32
The Genesis of Illness 37
Diseases 42
False Healings 47
The Devil and Disease 50
Conditions of Mystical Healing 54
Humility 62

CHAPTER II
Spiritual Correspondences 69

Gospel Quotes 71
Our Integrity 76
The Vocation of the Twelve 77
The Conduct of Missionaries 85
Divine Things and Public Opinion 89

The Spoken Word 95
Spiritual Families 97
Who is My Mother? Who are my Brothers? 99

CHAPTER III
Reception of Grace 107

Gospel Quotes 109
The Centurion 113
The Widow's Son 116
Where is Christ? 120
Driving Forces 125
The Messengers 128
The Cause of Fall 129
Preaching the Word 135
The Precursor 138
Penitence 143
The Evolution of Mysticism 150
Vigilance 155
The Gospel and Intelligence 157
Our Contemporaries 162
The Kingdom of God, Space, and Time 167
The Son of the Centurion 175
Regarding the Supernatural 179

CHAPTER IV
The Kingdom of Heaven 185

Gospel Quotes 187
The Imitation of Jesus 193
Mary Magdalene 199
The Flotsam and Jetsam 209
Divine Love 215
The Faith That Saves 217
The Function of Faith 226
Divine Clairvoyance 238
What Are Parables For? 242
The Parable of the Sower 248
Parables of the Grain 258
Final Parables 259

Acknowledgments

The publisher is deeply indebted to the "friends" of *Les Amitiés Spirituelles*, who have kept Paul Sédir's books in print in French for over a century, and for the dedication of those who have nurtured the vision that one day these books might appear in worthy editions for Anglophone readers. We gratefully thank in this connection Piers Vaughn and Peter Urbanski for the exchange of textual materials many years ago that led to this presents series, Robert Ledwidge for his technical assistance, and especially Madame Zadah Guérin-McCaffery, who nurtured this same vision and worked towards its realization for decades. Her skilled devotion to Sédir's works helped ensure that Sédir's carefully crafted style has been preserved in these Friends in Spirit translations.

Biographical Sketch

VON LE LOUP, son of Hippolyte Le Loup and Séraphine Foeller, was born on January 2, 1871 in Dinan, in the Côtes du Nord region of France. As a child, Yvon suffered the effects of tuberculosis, partial blindness, and a grave leg fracture that troubled him throughout his life. His mother, of Hessian origin, taught him German, which he later spoke fluently. At the age of nine, he made his First Communion at St Augustin's church, then entered the Jesuit school on rue des Francs Bourgeois, where he quickly distinguished himself by his great intelligence. Observant to a fault, he became a fine draughtsman and would have liked to paint. He was drawn to music, drawing, literature, and was extraordinarily dexterous with his hands. In due course, however, he was obliged to pursue a more practical academic course, owing to the influence of his father, an old soldier imbued with discipline who had little understanding for the refinement of this quiet child with lofty aspirations. And so, as soon a Yvon passed his academic exams (1892), he joined the Banque de France. He was twenty-one years old.

A few years earlier, in his late teens (around 1890), a profound shift in Yvon's orientation had taken shape. Not far from the Banque de France was an esoteric bookshop and publishing house (La Librairie du Merveilleux), where Yvon soon met the well-known writer on esoteric matters, Dr. Gerard Encausse (Papus). This led to a great friendship between the two quite different men. Papus set the young Yvon to work organizing his extensive esoteric library and introduced him to numerous personalities from the heady, even feverish, esoteric milieu of the time. One evening, he was taken to the home of Stanislas de Guaita, a nobleman of Italian descent who possessed the most complete esoteric library then in existence. Around this time, Yvon published an article ("An Experiment in Practical Occultism") and made his debut as a speaker on the theme: "Divinatory Sciences and Chiromancy."

In 1891, Papus had formed the Order of Martinists, based on the teachings of "The Unknown Philosopher," Louis Claude de Saint-Martin (1743–1803), and asked Yvon to collaborate. This fraternity took up the ideas of Martinez de Pasqually's Kabbalistic rite, and formed the first initiatory level of Guaita's Rosicrucian fraternity. In these circles, young authors frequently used pseudonyms. Yvon took the name Paul Sédir (anagram of désir), Gerard Encausse became Papus, Dr. Emmanuel Lalande used the name Marc Haven, etc. From the time of his association with the new Martinist Order, Yvon regularly published his work as Paul Sédir.

In 1895, Papus passed his doctorate in medicine and opened a home for the aged. This necessitated Sédir taking on the bulk of the esoteric-hermetic activities on which he and Papus had been collaborating. Every evening he gave classes in Hebrew and Sanskrit, the psychic training of Hindu fakirs, yoga, experimental alchemy, astrology, esoteric botany, etc. He also organized various research groups on related subjects.

Sédir was also much attracted to mysticism, and frequented literary circles such that of the poet Paul-Marie

Biographical Sketch

Verlaine. Meanwhile, in the rue de l'Ancienne Comédie, meetings of the Martinist Order were taking place, where Sédir became acquainted with individuals engaged in experiments regarding which he would later say: "It is here-below that you pay the highest price." His alchemical research did, however, enable him to acquire an ever deeper understanding of the foundations of what is known as the Great Work.

All these early aspects of Sédir's esoteric life reveal an overarching quest for truth that always led him to first experience something before speaking about it. He had by now attained great heights of "secret" knowledge, and even power. But to his great good fortune he had the wisdom to detach himself from these as soon as he realized their worthlessness and danger.

In July 1897, Gerard Encausse arranged for Sédir (then 26 years old) to meet a most singular man, Master Philippe of Lyon (Nizier Anthelme Philippe), to whom he was introduced by Madame Encausse. Master Philippe was a remarkable healer whom Sédir and others in his circle considered a Christian Master of the highest degree. Shortly after this meeting, Sédir left for Lyon to spend his vacation there. Just what happened at that time remains a private matter, although Sédir gives some inkling of what transpired in his autobiographical book *Initiations*, and also in a remarkable letter of May 1910:

> Together with some companions, I have done the rounds of all esotericisms and explored all crypts with the most fervent sincerity and hope of success. But none of the certainties I eventually grasped appeared

THE HEALINGS OF CHRIST

> to be The Certainty. Rabbis communicated their secret manuscripts to me; alchemists admitted me to their laboratories; Sufis, Buddhists, and Taoists led me during long nights to the abodes of their gods; a Brahmin let me copy his tables of mantra; a yogi imparted to me the secrets of contemplation. But one evening, after a certain meeting, what these admirable men taught became for me like haze rising at dusk on a sultry day. We run after what we think is hidden, but know nothing of our own religion, though its dogma and liturgy are the most complete presentation of integral knowledge on earth. Everything is there in Christianity. The Hindu *trimurti* is neither the Christian trinity nor the Pythagorean ternary; gnosis and the gospels do not lead to the same goal. Read in the texts what is there, not what one would wish to find there. To see that we know nothing; to experience that we can do nothing; to verify that heaven is here within us, and that our Friend constantly enfolds us within his blessed arms—this is the lesson of Jesus. This I have attempted to say by publishing, among other works, five volumes of lectures on the gospels.

Master Philippe had changed Sédir's orientation. *His mission had been affirmed.* He gave up all the esoteric fraternities (and his various ranks and offices in them) in order to devote himself wholly to living and spreading the gospel. His commentaries on the life of Christ are especially notable in that he accepts the intuitive faculty as a means of approaching the Truth. Sédir's literary output was extensive. His best known works are from this period are: *Prayer, Initiations, Mystic Forces, Christian Mysticism, Seven Mystical Gardens, The Childhood of Jesus, The Sermon on the Mount,*

Biographical Sketch

Some Friends of God, The Healings of Christ, The Kingdom of God, The Crowning of His Work, Weekly Meditations, and *The Incandescent Path.* His lectures and books drew many devoted students, and in due course a fellowship called Les Amitiés Spirituelles ("Friends in Spirit") was formed. This organization undertook to publish many of Sédir's books, and though it is much diminished, it remains active today.

Sédir died in Paris. Twenty years later, Breton poet and novelist Théophile Briant of Dinan wrote:

> On February 3, 1926, Paul Sédir died in Paris at the age of 55. The death of this admirable man, with his gospel-inspired heart, went almost unnoticed by the mainstream press, which was more preoccupied with crowning the charlatans and histrionics who were entertaining the public, even as international catastrophes were on the verge of breaking out. Apart from the chosen few whom this Apostle of the End Times had called to the Light, most post-war jabberers were unaware that one of the century's most eloquent voices was no longer to be heard. His was a forerunner's voice, the voice of a herald proclaiming in a wilderness of contentious crowds, a voice that had been devoted for years to spreading the gospel and, at the threshold of the abyss, was raised in dire warning against the multiplied prostitutions of the word.†

---

† This sketch is based on biographical materials provided by Émile Besson and Max Camis (close friends of Sédir), recently published in English in *Paul Sédir: His Life and Work* (Friends in Spirit, 2024).

Introduction

"Blessed, O my God, who gives me the quintessence
As a divine healing of our impurities,
And as the infinitely finer and purer essence
Which adds savor to our holy sensualities!

"I know there is a sorrow in the Soul's confessing
That shall never bite the hateful hollow Hells,
That, so as to weave my mystical crown by God's
  own blessing
The Universe and Time must render up their spells.

"These, Lord, are for the Spirits of all our Sages
That give us signs of our own dignity,
This intolerable howling of the inevitable ages
That merge and surge and emerge in Eternity!"

CHARLES BEAUDELAIRE

REATED BEINGS come into the world so as to fulfill a definite work. But, as an intimate, fraternal relationship cements them together like the stones of a universal temple, and as they are unable to reach the goal of their task without the help of one another, it falls to those who have finished their task first to come to the assistance of the loiterers. Thus, the collective "Great Work" (transmutation) can only be achieved through the perfect cooperation of generous efforts.

THE HEALINGS OF CHRIST

This is so, because each being carries within himself the desire to grow, which he tries to satisfy without being concerned about the bother it might cause his neighbors. These in turn, possessed of the same desire, do not take any precautions either. Moreover, through intuitive knowledge, we know the method of attaining a harmonious and innocent development. This method is that of moral law. But we do not obey it. Our disobedience creates our "sufferings," and it is our obstinacy that makes us confuse their origin with the origin of evil. In fact, through the annoyances we cause each other to bear, we both learn how to moderate our selfishness.

God could only have created the world for his good, since this world is not necessary to him. God can be nothing but All-Goodness. The evils of life are but evils to those who endure them. Of themselves, they are only the means used to make us evolve—because no one, not even a stone, can live or grow without absorbing some weaker living particles, and without suffering therefrom.

This process, which seems distressing at first, is assuaged when within us a vista opens into the mystic universe where providence reigns. It is then that we fathom the true characteristics of suffering and of its spiritualizing results. It is then that we become aware that its angels know how deeply they have to dig their furrows—and we come to the rather surprising experience of finding out that ordeals are cruel only in the measure that we repulse them. Because, in the measure wherein we accept them, we are assimilated into the eternal being of the perpetual Martyr and his powerful energies. In us, the self alone suffers: the body is sensitive only through the virtues of soul life with which it is saturated; the soul remains the impassible witness. The soul

Introduction

is the divine spark, and so it does not sin. It might be said that it is the envelope or cloak of the spirit—the self, the personality—that wants to disobey or obey. It is that envelope which ascends or descends, which suffers, and upon which true healing operates. Hence it is imperative to elevate the self, to extract it from the world where selves tear one another apart, to transplant it into the world where selves become the servants of each other. This transplantation is a transmutation, whose alchemist is named Jesus.

We are spirit and matter. Whether matter enchains the spirit or the spirit elevates matter, there always occurs a disaggregation of the one or a disorganization of the other—of which suffering is the consequence. These alternating dominations finally purify the evil that swarms in us. Therefore, suffering must be redemptive; it is a spark of Jesus.

Why does God allow evil? Why does he permit all the horrors among which we struggle? A host of thinkers, with much ingenuity, have tried to solve this enigma. No philosophical answer has yet been able to stop the frightful chorus of this universal complaint.

Religious answers, on their own, lull a few patient ones to sleep. And a few superhuman souls have conquered the fear of suffering, and on account of that victory have already found permanent happiness on earth.

Thinkers, who see nature as nothing but an immense battlefield of divergent forces and interests, estimate that the solution of this problem can only be solved through a more profound knowledge of ethnic, social, and scientific laws, or by a wiser understanding of the interconnections that link the individual to the collectivity. Positivists are of the view that after many centuries natural evolution will of itself bring these results.

THE HEALINGS OF CHRIST

Deists, who acknowledge the hypothesis of a supreme being, are divided into two camps. The one camp sees in the universe nothing but the progressively more material emanations of this first motive power—but this power cannot intervene in the functioning of cosmic laws, since these laws constitute part of its own biology. Looked at this way, everything is ruled with mathematical justice. On this account, for the other camp the hypothesis of multiple lives becomes plausible—that is, creatures are the only responsible authors of their sufferings, which take on the character, not of penalties, but of payment due for the prior thefts of which the culprits were guilt by transgressing the implacable laws of life.

Other spiritually-minded people admit that the primordial cause is independent of its work, which it could have dispensed from fulfilling. They do not believe in the emanation, but in the creation, of the world, because, were God not free, he would not be God. This system, whose most perfect form is to be found and explicated in the first verses of John's gospel (and later developed in Catholic theology), teaches us that in God are contained, not only everything that is imaginable, but much besides that is situated far beyond the reach of our intelligence or sensibility. This same God could have created the world entirely different from that which it is, or not have created the world at all, or else might have created other worlds *ad infinitum*. The possibility here is that there might be many other kinds of universes than ours.

The upshot of this last consideration is that any creature, whatever or whoever it might be, always finds itself entirely subject to Divine goodwill. This conclusion, although it remains indemonstrable, nevertheless seems to be the only

Introduction

one offering the possibility of infinite developments for beings, spares them from despair, and makes them capable of ever-surpassing themselves. Because, why would God, to whom no one is essential, have taken the trouble to fashion our person, if not for our own advantage? Because of his love, God is good: he is perfect love. Therefore, in him we will find all succor, all powers, and all knowledge. Hence, the ordeals and annoyances on our path, whether they be the just results of our prior follies or the unjust efforts of wickedness thereabouts, ought to appear to us essentially as work prepared for our personal evolution by a very wise and loving Master. God, Infinite Goodness, never becomes irritated with us, does not punish us, does not avenge himself. He only lets us bear the painful reaction of our disobediences every time we turn a deaf ear to his voice. Does the student know the plans his teacher has in mind for his future? Is the soldier informed of the general's plans of campaign?

Within the universal enclosure, where time, space, and conditions are the governing factors, any movement provokes its opposite. Over the expanse of this immense battlefield, all creatures struggle and develop their powers for personal growth, just as does the studious adolescent who hopes to obtain his diploma. But the true result of his application will be that of having developed a fine, concise, and rich intelligence for himself—something much more useful than any diploma. So, in the school of the world, created beings, without really being aware of it, construct for themselves these marvelous faculties that religious authors disclose to us when they speak of virtues by the exercise of which nature and society are being slowly transformed in the direction of a permanent harmony and a universal peace.

THE HEALINGS OF CHRIST

Besides, these sufferings we believe to be unjust—do they not appear to be so merely because of the impossibility we find ourselves in to determine their primal cause? Even admitting that this earth alone is inhabited, where would we find a mind perspicacious enough to follow the chain of the determining factors of a tragedy back to just its thirtieth or fortieth link? And if, in accord with the immense crowd of those who have believed and do now believe in an invisible universe, we try to uncover in the occult world the mysterious forces that cause such or such material catastrophe, would we not very shortly have to admit our incapacity? Moreover, if we knew the mysteries, if we knew what we face when we disobey the law or commit evil, would our wisdom be anything but a selfish calculation? Could it lead us as high and as far as we want to go—where we feel we should go?

Since it is God who has created us, it is from him that we come, and it is to him that we must return—and the force that brought us down here is the same force that must bring us back to him. We know that this force is love and not knowledge, love and not power: love—sire of all knowledge and power. Hence, if we strain every fiber of our being towards him who sent us, we return to him. And as we rise, the clouds dissipate proportionately.

God is the Master; it is from him that we receive the very force for our revolts. But, if we get scratched while leaping over a hedge while out marauding, we have no one to blame but ourselves. St Bernard of Clairvaux, who knew men and stirred their souls, said: "Let man give up his own will, and hell will cease to exist." Simple words these, upon which we must meditate a long time to fathom their depths. Yes, we are the sole cause of our suffering. We are our own execu-

Introduction

tioners because, had we not given him the means first, no being has the power or the right to hurt us. Undeniably a hard and bitter statement: but it is often needful to tell oneself the bitter truth.

The exact meaning of the word "sin" is: transgression, or infraction of the law. Moral law is identical to divine law, and experience shows that the latter is but the ensemble of the universal laws of life. In sin, there has to be disobedience and infraction, moral perversity, and some material bungling. This artlessness may be remedied through material losses, illnesses, or misfortunes; but to erase the perversity demands a moral agent known as contrition.

Having heard this word from childhood on may have eroded its impact on us. In reality, contrition is a drama of pathos. It begins in remorse, is strengthened by repentance, and attains full intensity through penance.

Contrition means "shattering": it is the hard stone of the self shattered by the ardor of repentance and gnawed by the expiatory bitterness of tears. Similar to the flint, this self conceals a secret fire in its core—imperceptible just now, able to set the world afire tomorrow and engulf the mightiest forces. This fire is the spark of the Word, the seed of eternal life: our soul. Repentance is its first ignition. Moreover, the harder the heart has become, the greater the violence when it shatters; the deeper its sinks into remorse, the higher it springs towards impending atonements. Thus does the soul show the ugliness of evil to the self. And if the self recognizes this ugliness, the repentant heart reascends to God. True contrition saves us from despair. It solicits us towards life, towards intense activity. The great doers, the launchers of the impossible, were almost always penitents of old, rather than merely ambitious men.

THE HEALINGS OF CHRIST

There is in repentance an inconceivably contagious emotion. Sometimes we see a mother who, touched by the tears of her child, forgives him, and then, loving him twice as much as before, exerts in his behalf all sorts of avenues of devotion. Read again the parable of the prodigal son. Heaven does much more, and proves itself far more indulgent, than the most loving of mothers. Read again the story of Mary Magdalene, and as well that concerning the shepherd looking for his lost sheep. I repeat: the Father loves us. He is not a haughty and distant God. He loves us with tenderness, with adorable solicitude, and has the delightful trait of coming down to our level—something only perfect affection could bring about.

The necessity to act urges us implacably on. It constitutes the school for our liberty, the method for our total growth. At all times, before us stand a form of good and a form of evil: one silent and veiled, the second fascinating or seductive, because evil has no any scruples about winning followers, whereas good always respects our free will.

If only we listened to our conscience with the conviction of its infallibility, we could become perfect without suffering. But we are hardheaded. We obstinately believe ourselves wiser than God. And our most painful experiences hardly suffice in convincing us that we are ourselves well and truly the authors of our torments. Thus, the ordeal is a recall to order and a remedy that patiently sculpts the marvelous statue we will one day become. God does not want us to suffer. He only wants us to get to work. Yet we chose, either by malice or stubbornness, the manner of working that provokes suffering—rather than that by which we

Introduction

could realize the same works and the same progress through joy and in serenity. Let us remember the call of Jesus: "Come to me, you who are weary and heavy-laden, and I shall comfort you." God has never wanted to torment us. He only wants us to perfect ourselves.

Any act cast into the world-arena is a seed—a seed that not only is indestructible but multiplies itself with ever-increasing fecundity. Both good and evil become stronger and stronger with the passage of time. It is only to be expected, then, that the older the wrong-doing, the more complicated it becomes to atone for it. Explaining the problem of suffering through the theory that such is the way wrongdoings committed in past lives are paid for, has been tried. But this hypothesis only postpones the solution. Whether there be but one single incarnation on earth, or several; whether there be past and future transmigrations upon other planets (hypotheses the Church has never condemned anyway); whether we suffer for ourselves alone or as holocaust for the faults of some of our brothers; whether we suffer only to make amends for our personal sins; whether providence subjects us to these sufferings in order to develop our unknown faculties; whether our individual destiny is part of the collective destiny of our race or country—regardless how all that may be, the basis of the problem remains. And since that basis consists of inaccessible facts, we have to accept our suffering, and our knowing nothing about it, until we have attained the mystical summit from where the entire world can be seen.

The injustices we revolt against only appear to be injustices. Who can flatter himself of having discovered all the causes of even the simplest fact? Who can tell if the scoundrels and wrongdoers who cash in on everything do not

THE HEALINGS OF CHRIST

owe their apparent happiness to an unsuspected pact contracted between their spirit and some temporal gods; and if they will not someday have to disgorge their ill-gotten gains? Does not apparent happiness often hide some great sorrow? Who knows if the good people who so often lead unfortunate lives are not subjected to their sufferings in order to develop patience, resignation, and faith in an ideal. Or rather, might they not be suffering for another too blind to learn his lesson from the ordeal? Who knows if they might not have the privilege of paying their own debts immediately, or at least of paying their spiritual debts in the shortest time possible?

Because our immortal self chose the path of least effort and lagged behind before it accepted God and Christ, from the day it saw the light an imperious desire awakened within it to make up for lost time. The self, now recognizing the value of time, perceives the glorious horizons of its spiritual future, and for that end might choose to accept—might even demand—a period of intensive work. The earthly self knows nothing of these dramas. But its ignorance, which at first seems cruel to us, on the contrary procures for it magnificent results. That is because the self, in order to go beyond itself, must surpass that same self and escape into the free world of the spirit where faith reigns, where all worries cease to exist, where one breathes immutable peace and invincible energy.

The mystic is the greatest optimist. The mystic has the strongest will. The true mystic is the most active doer. The mystic is all these things because he lives in the eternal, and only there does the meaning of all enigmas and the absolute value of all obstacles appear.

Whatever theory we adopt, we must accept suffering. No

Introduction

debtor pays his debts by denying them. The less personal the aims or motives for our efforts, the purer, nobler, and more prolific they are. Look for Christ!

⊕

Why need we shrink our concepts? Do not true scientists concede that imagination has the most fruitful role in the discovery of hypotheses; that it may in one swoop clarify a whole set of events and permit their classification? Imagination is nothing but the mirror (too often tarnished) wherein are reflected invisible landscapes. Why, then, limit life to this little globe? Why should not the other worlds be inhabited? We cannot know anything of their biology, except by induction from what we have so far discovered of terrestrial physics and chemistry. Of interplanetary space we know nothing. We are ignorant of how thermodynamics act in zodiacal space. Astronomy rests upon the hypothesis that everything in the cosmos follows the same pattern as that of the earth—a most unlikely hypothesis, indeed, to the philosopher. Any other hypothesis is permissible.

Whether or not we accept the theory of multiple lives, whether or not we admit that planets are inhabited by similar or dissimilar creatures than those on earth, we must at least agree that each one of us receives—down to the least details of our life, and from all corners of the universe—billions upon billions of corporeal and soul influences, only a small part of which rises to the surface of our consciousness. What conclusion can we draw from this infinite interplay? How can we guess what will be the possible effects of even one lone gesture of ours, which the elasticity of imponderable interconnections causes to rebound through space, only to have it recoil inevitably upon us through the centuries?

THE HEALINGS OF CHRIST

As the intellectual universe and the moral universe have far more sensibility and are far more impressionable than the material universe, how much time might it take to right a wrong? Do not these complexities make the redressing of such grievances that much more difficult and take that much more time? Would we not simplify our future, even our near future, were we to live with a deeper sense of moral responsibility?

It does not seem possible to reject suffering, or to escape from it, except temporarily. Listen to the tales of woe of drug addicts who have taken the cure! Let us look at the inner deserts of selfish people who have petrified their hearts. Most of us are content to submit to suffering; a few try to escape from it; others ask for it. Let us first consider the mean in this respect.

Unhappy people at first revolt. Then they learn how to bear their fate stoically, through nobility of soul. Later, they are made aware of religious perspectives and of the immense benefits of expiations accepted willingly. Finally, the folly of the Cross takes them up to the mystical heavens of voluntary sacrifice. But to breathe such rarefied air, a long period of training is obligatory. Let us, then, make use of the lessons, even the easiest ones, that each day offers us. All contain a light.

> Almighty love gives to the creature
> The meaning of his misfortune,
> Which leads to repentance
> By a slow and high road, but very sure. (Verlaine)

Introduction

But let enthusiasts beware of excesses. When we are ill, the body must be attended to. We must attempt to overcome our sorrow. If we are not healed, if our tears fall in spite of us, the test of suffering will nevertheless bear spiritual fruits. Did not Jesus, in his advance compassion for our weaknesses, speak as if he too were weak? Without concern for scandalizing stoical pride, did he not say to the Father: "May this cup pass from me, if it be possible"? Truthfully, it takes more courage for us to assuage our bodily pains and dry our tears as though we could only rely on ourselves (even while surrendering ourselves with both strength and abandonment into God's hands) than it does to let ourselves fall without resistance under the heavy blows of fate.

Those who are spiritually inclined tend to believe that a general and vague sentimentality suffices to accomplish their duty. They are wrong. It is particularly on the mystical paths that energy, courage, and vigorous will-power are indispensable. Whenever some sorrow comes our way, we must not desire for its end. Although of course using reasonable means to make it cease, still we must accept the suffering with a smile. We do not know if others are suffering as much, or far more, than we do. Has not our Master suffered, and is he not still suffering, and will he not suffer infinitely more until the end of the world?

The better we use the present, the more beautiful will the oncoming future be. If we attain the state of serene, joyous patience, of perfect acceptance, in exchange we receive the inalterable peace of silent union with the Master of dolor and of beatitude.

Selfishness has so anchored its roots into our very depths —from the marrow of our bones to the highest summits of our spirit—that, to uproot them, to yank them out, we

THE HEALINGS OF CHRIST

need almost infinite patience. First, let us learn not to complain. To groan, means to weaken. So let us not be impatient, or distracted. Let us not beg for sympathy, or relate our woes in detail. If you want to grow, if you want the strong remedy to take its effect, do not go to any creature for succor—take refuge only with the supernatural Physician. When he attempts to heal you, it is because he loves you. No one in the world loves you as he does. He too weeps when he sees you suffer.

When sorrow becomes unbearable, lock yourselves in, weep, moan in solitude, pray for hours or days on end if need be, but appear among your fellow beings only when you have regained a calm countenance. You think such an effort impossible? No, many have borne it. You think it useless? No effort is useless, this one particularly, because, among all others, at the cost of your tears, it adjusts itself magnificently to the dignity of your soul.

In truth, our tears belong to God alone: they belong to the Father because they are alive; they belong to the Son because they save us; they belong to the Spirit because they evoke peace; they belong to the Virgin because they are sources of humility. They must never be shed, save in the most secret crypt of our heart, and in the night of our self-will; springboard to stars, they shed hope upon unsurmised despair.

The practice of suffering procures us strength because it reveals to us our weakness. The condition for becoming stronger is to recognize that we are weak. Suffering transmutes our natural debility into supernatural vigor, and the vampire of doubt into creative faith. Doubt is the mortal poison of energy, the virulent octopus of the will. We have to build some kind of faith for ourselves. No matter what

Introduction

kind it is, it is preferable to eclecticism, dilettantism, or scepticism. But we must choose the finest motive for pursuing a course: obedience out of love.

Armed with this force, we will definitively triumph. All suffering being equal, it is the atheist who suffers most, because in this poor wretch torments retain their dissolving virtues: the aridity of soul that seeps into him dries up his precious energies, whereas the martyr to an idea (even a mediocre one) is sustained by a secret joy, and his sacrifice always makes fruitful some fallow ground of the moral world. Suffering endured out of love always engenders a spiritual expansion before which the doors of beatitudes open wide. Then begins the labor of apostleship.

Let us remain humble too, since we can accomplish nothing without receiving help secretly. So let us chase away all worries. Or better still, let us look at them as a passing spectacle. Finally, let us not cling to our likes and dislikes, or our projects, cost what it may. If we place whatever good there is in them "into the Father's hands," the Son will find a thousand means of not letting it go sterile. Let us do everything possible. However, since the chains of the possible are elastic, when all things seem to abandon us, let us abandon everything to God.

On the other hand, we must guard against any excess of zeal. We must not seek suffering for the pleasure of conquering it—for that is pride. Christ never said: "Suffer to please me." On the contrary, he said: "Come to me, you who are heavy-laden and weary, and I shall comfort you." He said: "Take up my yoke and learn of me that I am kind and lowly of heart; and you shall find rest unto your soul, for my yoke is easy and my burden is light." He also said: "Whoever wants to save his soul, loses it." There is also this

THE HEALINGS OF CHRIST

parable for the impatient: "Who is the king, who, going to war against another king, does not first sit and ponder to find out if he, with ten thousand men, can go to encounter the one who comes with twenty thousand men?" Hence, it is not suffering, but how to overcome suffering, that should be our concern.

⊕

Just as a seed entrusted to the earth undergoes, through the dissolving action of physical-chemical agents, a profound decomposition before sprouting roots and stems, before ripening and reproducing itself a hundredfold, so too the self must be entrusted to the earth, undergo suffering, see itself torn apart by the fire of pain, the water of tears, the snows of ingratitudes—so that it might be reborn, transfigured by the rays of the supernatural star.

Suffering thus understood bears marvelous fruits. There is no asceticism, no contemplation, no iron will, not even a vast intellect, that can procure true knowledge, force, and self-mastery as well as suffering does. The perfectly patient man masters himself and conquers the world. Still better, he earns the friendship of Christ and certain beatitude. Purgatories, no matter where we suffer them, elevate us as high as they have precipitated us low. Fear nothing: the light within us is immortal. You can hide it or adulterate it, of course, but kill it?—never. It is life, the mystical blood of the world, the universal medicine. It aggregates the whole human species into one sole organism. Through the virtue of this mysterious unity, each individual is affected by the suffering of all that dissolves in the mass, carrying along the seeds of compassion, and prepares therein the blossoming of the roses of Christly love.

Introduction

Suffering patiently borne purifies both heart and body, unfolds humility, optimism, and the spirit of prayer. But one must not be surprised if the true servants of God suffer more. The greater our thirst for heaven, the faster the spirit advances on the narrow path; and in the same space of time one meets a great many spiritual obstacles that are translated in the physical world as ordeals or tests. I am speaking here not of the Platonic Christians who merely offer their pious desires to heaven, but of the active Christians who want to act, and who do act.

Each sorrow is a partial death, prelude to a rebirth. Any moral fault, localized physically in one of our organs that is subjected to suffering, dies and is reborn a virtue. That is why the capacity to suffer is the measure of moral vigor.

Progress does not advance in a straight line. It is a liberation. When one pushes on one side with all one's might and then as far as possible in the opposite direction, by dint of excess in all directions the being reaches his equilibrium. Misfortune also brings happiness, sorrow, or joy. But as we misuse happiness, as we fall asleep in joy, other ordeals spring forth. And then come new joys. We become tender, soft; we acquire calm, because goodness—the visage of eternal perfection—always surpasses evil in the end. One by one, we experience the lacunae of intelligence and the weaknesses of the will. Then we are ultimately, but kindly, driven back to God, the only recourse; and at last we perceive the Redeemer. Without Christ, suffering would be but payment due. With him, suffering becomes a transfiguring force.

Interrogate the sublimest voices earth has ever heard; they unanimously proclaim the nobility of sacrifice. Hence, there exists outside of ourselves an objective Ideal, an Entity

THE HEALINGS OF CHRIST

representative of altruism and devotion. This God of Light often seems to be weaker than the god of selfishness. But, since the very essence of love is to give itself, this apparently vanquished one is in reality the conqueror. Christ is the incarnation of this love. Interwoven with the masses in creation, informed of all that happens to them through the exquisite refinement of his spiritual organism, attentive to all their problems and hopes because of his most tender compassion, he has been able to state in all truth that whatsoever we give to the unfortunate, we have given to him. Each patient being, no matter in what corner of immense nature he conceals himself, communicates with him all the more intimately because he suffers with resignation. And he communicates with him that much more effectively because his sufferings are devoid of selfishness.

At a certain stage, when personal sufferings have reached an end, our concern for others grows, and with "ineffable sighs" our spirit asks for supplementary ordeals. It is then that we enter into the career of apostolate: we are less and less preoccupied with our own destiny; our whole concern from then on is to bring to the same Shepherd, who has healed and comforted us, the still-erring sheep:

> Christly sorrow is immense,
> Like the human heart;
> She suffers, then thinks,
> And calmly goes her way;
> She stands on Calvary,
> Full of tears and without cries:
> She also is a mother,
> But what a mother, and of what a son!"
> (Verlaine)

Introduction

Contrary to the teachings of philosophers, being "superhuman" does not mean that we must become impassible to base, gross, or futile sorrows, but that we diminish their occurrence and undertake to purify ourselves nobly. An ideal is only true when noble. Tears are precious. So let us beware of drying up their divine source, or of shedding them for unworthy causes. Only hearts ravaged by inflexible, inexorable pain can ever feel the refreshing breath of the spirit. Suffering exalts and regenerates those alone.

What does one really have to fear? Does not contemporary science instruct the positivist in the conservation of all energies? What more imperious motive, then, could there be, for the one who believes only in matter, to overcome all suffering?—given that, according to this view, his own forces will not die with him but will on the contrary augment the imponderable heritage of his family, of his race, and of the whole of humanity? And as for the believer, does he not already have the certitude that his resistances to sorrow not only will live with him, but will be harvested by God, the great Martyr, so as to be transmuted and then showered as marvelous benedictions upon the whole world?

We must exercise ourselves to look upon the enemies of our apparent happiness, not as enemies, but as loyal adversaries whose strength remains always proportionate to ours, and who, as soon as we begin to fight, are unable to do us any harm, since the actual harm would be, precisely, *not* to fight.

⊕

One of the most common complaints is that of illness. According to physicians, everyone carries within himself a disease, or the germ of all diseases. It has also been ascertained that the causes of diseases are of a physiological and an atavistic order; later, we will find them again as belonging to a moral and a spiritual order. We will do all we can to study the problem of disease deeply from its inmost viewpoint.

When examining the march of the world, one discovers an immanent justice that compels creatures to pay for their flagrant digressions. Without wasting too much time to explain this fact—either according to the Catholic theory of our living just one lifetime (during which illness is a test that develops the energies from which our personality is built), or else following the Eastern theory of multiple lives (according to which suffering is the reaction to the excesses committed during prior existences)—in either case, we will find how illness permits us to perfect our immortal part: our soul or our spirit.

Illness has a physical usefulness, as it teaches us hygiene, temperance, and how to care for the body. It has a moral usefulness, as it teaches us how to develop our energies. And it has as well a spiritual usefulness, which we will discuss later.

How should we act when illness overtakes us? First of all, by taking care of our body through all legitimate means, as it is our servant and a fine tool that, though only on loan, we must still perfect. Secondly (and contrary to the theory of unacceptable revolt now in vogue), bear the sickness with resignation. Jesus said: "Possess yourselves in patience," and the gospel is the very difficult and severe schooling to the fulfillment of this precept. Christ also said: "The kingdom of heaven belongs to the violent"—which means, to those who have developed true energy. Hence, when disease comes, let us suffer without complaint. Let us recognize at

Introduction

its inception that there is an immanent justice in it, and that no one suffers unjustly. Consequently, let us accept the lesson, while taking the best care of ourselves. That is the proper attitude of mind. It develops our spiritual forces and brings us closer to the kingdom of God.

Let us be aware that heaven often places us in the presence of the impossible, of the inevitable, in order to show us our weakness and our powerlessness before him who is the All-Powerful and All-Reality. All physicians find themselves at times before insoluble cases, for which there is but one recourse: call for the help of the great Healer, meaning: pray. Disease, then, brings us to the school of prayer, which leads us finally to the kingdom of light and peace.

While he suffers, the patient is brought to examine his self, to go over his past, and quite often to discover the culpable act that was the initial cause of the disease. This examination leads him to repent, to recognize his error, and to become humble. Humility is the indispensable condition for our progress. As our duty is to progress, we must maintain humility; we must nurture it in order to grow ever more deeply within.

It is not through chance that there are incurable diseases. There are beings who can pay their debts only through physical pain, because the quality of suffering is always proportionate to the quality of the one who bears it. Here again we observe that justice reigns. But this justice must not prevent us from doing everything possible to diminish that evil. Moreover, we must never criticize the sick person, who may be the opportune instrument of work for his family. We must never judge him, because that judgment could bring upon our head the taint from which he suffers. And should we be in the same situation, we might perhaps act

THE HEALINGS OF CHRIST

worse than he. Life sends us, in spite of ourselves, to a practical school, fertile in ensuing experiences. But whether we bear tests or pay debts, we cannot do it alone, without help. Illness brings us back to God, of whom we seldom think, because in life we believe we owe our success to our qualities. But these, after all, are nothing but gifts. And so, when examining the cause of our failures, we will note that they are usually due to our having too high an opinion of ourselves.

How then should we take care of our sick? We must consider them prefigurations of Christ, who said to us: "That which you do to the least of them, you do for me." This is an ever-present reality: a living reality. When, because of compassion, the Father sent his Son to save mankind, he meant for him to undergo all the forms of suffering on earth and upon all worlds. Jesus took upon himself almost all the sufferings of those he healed. His presence among us is still real: not one man suffers without Christ being near him, or without Christ shouldering part of that suffering. All we do to our neighbor, then, we do to Jesus.

Our work lies in compassion, in opening our heart. It is our heart that gives us our true worth. This is what we must yearn for. Let us welcome all beings and things with the same amenity, because they are one and all workers of God. Our present and urgent task is to open our heart to the work of real and practical fraternity, which some among you have already begun, and which I hope you will realize. It will be of great joy to me to be of use to you in any manner possible.

CHAPTER I

Mystical Healings

ESUS AND HIS disciples made their way to Capernaum. Here, as soon as the sabbath came, he entered into the synagogue and taught; and they were amazed by his teaching, for he sat there teaching them like one who had authority, not as the scribes.

In the synagogue was a man who was possessed by an unclean spirit, that cried aloud: "Why dost thou meddle with us, Jesus of Nazareth? Hast thou come to make an end of us? I recognize thee for what thou art: the Holy One of God." Jesus rebuked it: "Silence," he said; "Come out of him."

Then the unclean spirit set the man into a convulsion; throwing him violently to the floor, he cried with a loud voice, and went out of him without doing him any injury. The terrified spectators were astonished. They asked one another: "What can this be? This is a new teaching. See how he has authority and power to lay his command even on the unclean spirits, and they obey him!" His fame and the story of his doings immediately spread throughout the whole region of Galilee.

As soon as they had left the synagogue, they went with James and John into the house of Simon and Andrew. The mother of Simon's wife was lying sick in bed, with a fever, and they made haste to tell Jesus of her; whereupon he went to her bedside, he took her by the hand, and lifted her up. All at once the fever left her, and she began ministering to them.

THE HEALINGS OF CHRIST

When evening came and the sun had set, they brought to him all those who were afflicted, even those who were possessed by devils, The whole city stood crowding there at the door. Laying hands upon each of them, Jesus healed them all, so that what the prophet Isaiah had announced would be accomplished: "He has taken our infirmities upon himself and shouldered our sicknesses."

Demons came out of many, crying aloud: "Thou art the Son of God!" But he rebuked them and forbade them to speak, for they knew that he was Christ.

Then, at very early dawn, he left them, and went away to a lonely place, and began praying there. Simon and his companions went in search of him; and when they found him, they told him: "All men are looking for thee." He answered them: "Let us go to the next country towns, so that I can preach there too; it is for this I have come." So he continued to preach in their synagogues and all through Galilee, and to cast out many devils.

A leper came up to him, asking for his aid; he knelt at his feet and said: "If it be thy will, thou hast power to make me clean." Jesus was moved with pity; he held out his hand and touched him, and said: "It is my will: be thou made clean." Whereupon the leprosy left him immediately and he was cleansed. Jesus sent him away then and there with the severe warning: "Be sure thou dost not speak of this to anyone, but show thyself to the priest, and bring the offering for thy cleansing which Moses ordained, as a testimony for them." But,

Mystical Healings

as soon as he had gone away, that man began to talk publicly and spread the story around, so that Jesus could no longer go into any of the cities openly, because the multitudes would come to listen to him and to be healed of their infirmities. But he went to dwell apart in the wilderness.

⊕

A few days later he returned to Capernaum. It was learned that he was in a house; and so many people gathered together that there was no room to receive them, not even at the door. Then there came people who brought a paralytic, carried by four men. As they could not come close to him because of the crowd, they uncovered the roof over the place where he was, and through the opening let down the bed where lay the paralytic. Jesus, seeing their faith, told him: "My child, thy sins are forgiven thee." Whereupon the Pharisees and scribes who were sitting there fell to reasoning thus: "How can this man talk so blasphemously? Who can forgive sins but God and God only."

Jesus knew of these secret thoughts of theirs, and said to them openly: "Why do you reason thus in your hearts? Which command is more lightly given, to say to the paralytic: 'Thy sins are forgiven thee,' or to say 'Rise up, take up thy bed and walk?' And now, to convince you that the Son of Man has power to forgive sins while he is on earth (here he spoke to the palsied man): I tell thee, arise, take up thy bed with thee and go home." The man rose at once in full sight of them, took up his bedding, and went home. All were stupe-

THE HEALINGS OF CHRIST

fied and, giving praise to God, said: "We have seen strange things, today." Then Jesus went again towards the sea. The multitudes came to him and he taught them.

✠

Then he went out, and caught sight of a publican, called Levi, son of Alphaeus, sitting at work in the customs house, and said to him, "Follow me." And he rose up, and left all behind, and followed him. Then Levi made a great feast for him in his house, and there was a crowded company of publicans and others who were their fellow-guests. But the scribes and Pharisees complained to his disciples, saying: "Why do you eat and drink with publicans and sinners?" Jesus answered them: "It is those who are sick, not those who are in health, that have need of the physician. I have not come to call the just; I have come to call sinners to repentance."

Then they said unto him: "How is it that thy disciples eat and drink, when John's disciple are always fasting and praying, and the Pharisees' disciples too?" He then said unto them, "Can you persuade the men of the bridegroom's company to fast, while the bridegroom is still with them? No, the days will come when the bridegroom shall be taken away from them; they will fast when that day comes."

He also told them this parable: "Nobody uses a piece taken from a new cloak to patch an old one; if that is done, he will have torn the new cloak, and the piece taken from the new one will not match the old. Nor does anybody put new wine into old wineskins; if that

Mystical Healings

is done, the new wine bursts the skins; the wine would spill and the skins would be spoilt. If the wine is new, it must be put into fresh wineskins, and so both are kept safe. Nobody who has been drinking old wine desires the new; he will tell you 'The old is better.'"[1]

The Mystical Healer

ESSENTIAL IN ORDER to heal by means of prayer are loyalty, calm, and benevolence; and in particular, one must remain in constant union with Christ—the supernatural Physician. This last condition completes and embodies all the others.

It is particularly in his relationship with women that the healer must show loyalty. Of all people, it is especially he, the healer, who must check, withhold, and break the ardor of the obscure forces of the ever-active animal instinct. He, above all, must remember that one sole glance of covetousness is effectively an adultery. Sick women who come to him are defenseless in two ways: they need help, and they must also place their confidence in him as if he were a superior being. Hence, he must beware of and guard against magnetic disturbances in himself, or in his female patient, twice, three, even seven times. The evil he would commit by utilizing his spiritual prestige to his own imagined benefit would be base, vile, and heavy-laden with endless repercussions.

The healer must have imperturbable calm: calm for himself, calm for his patients. More than any other method,

---

[1] Mark 1:21 to 2:22; Luke 4:33–44; 5:12–39; Matthew 8:2–4, 14–17; 9:1–17.

THE HEALINGS OF CHRIST

healing by prayer pulls the one who makes use of it towards the Invisible, towards the most secret, most unexplored regions of the Invisible, which for that very reason are the most abundant in surprises. The tension of prayer, to which the mystic constantly subjects himself, refines and sensitizes his spirit. More than any other man, he receives the whiplash of a great many events, good or evil—staged in the subtle worlds—that finally congeal upon our earth and its inhabitants. The higher the mystic ascends, the deeper he sinks into the depths; the more active are the forces that his spirit breathes and assimilates, the more disconcerting are their *modus operandi*. To keep his intellectual, soul, and physical equilibrium, the mystical healer has but one resource: composure, presence of mind, infinite prudence, perfect self-control.

The sick are far more subject than others to the penetration of invisible influences, though all unbeknownst to them. Their physiological disequilibrium makes them vulnerable. Their moral and physical sufferings are the episodes of their struggles against their invaders. The one whose sole means of healing is prayer must therefore prove twice as calm and strong as the sick (for himself and for them)—that is, for all they lack in equilibrium and resistance. Especially in our time, do not sanction your patients' speaking of magic or claiming to be the victims of occult practices—primarily because it is rarely true, and then again, because it is in any case preferable to prevent them from engrossing themselves in such notions. If you need to say a few words to your patients, either alone or in public, never speak of occultism or sorcery, even from a theoretical standpoint; indeed, forbid the topic.

In the third place, be kind. May the great, indispensable

Mystical Healings

precept of brotherly love be constantly before your heart and will: pure, fraternal love, devoid of familial selfishness, devoid of any intellectual interest or sentimental prestige. It must be love of the spirit. Be as concerned about each patient as you would be about yourself. Find the word that will comfort them, the gesture that will soothe them. Treat them with serene kindness. Forget their impatience or lack of common sense. Forgive and forget their ingratitude. Give up your comfort to satisfy their perhaps petty despotisms. Never miss praying for the wretched ones. Remember: it is by arduous labor at the forge that one becomes a blacksmith. Do not argue, do not quarrel, do not scorn. Do not pry overmuch into whether something is traceable to alcoholism or debauchery. See only the suffering flesh, the being in distress. Be kind as the Father is to everyone, everywhere, in everything. No vociferous joviality, no frowning brow. Just smile. Greet everyone as welcome guests, since they are to be the instruments for you to work with, which means they are occasions for you to help our Master. Let his joy, when witnessing your obedience, be your joy, be your happiness. Become blissful. Remain in the cheerfulness of the slaves to love, and you will radiate effortlessly, you will transmute the despair around you.

Finally, be united, live in unity, remain in a state of union. Before lifting a finger, before saying a word or looking around, check whether your hand, your tongue, your eyes are with Jesus. There should be no slander, no blame (not even in the intonation of your voice), no unnecessary words. Do not express anything about any person who is absent except as you would were they present. Do not say anything unkind about animals, objects, or the weather; about anyone or anything. Think only of Christ. Live only for Christ. Obey only the voice of Christ in your conscience. Act as best you can. Feed the self with aliments repugnant to it. Help everything living to live. Go towards the timid, also the shameless, also the poor. Jesus told his disciples: "Fear not, I shall be with you every day till the end of time." Be that kind of disciple.

You will see people with incurable diseases healed. Do not be surprised: kneel down and give him thanks. You will see insignificant illnesses resistant to your prayers and your spiritual fasts: again, do not be surprised: kneel down and become as naught. Perhaps you will be led into frightful hells. Maybe angels will take you up to ineffable ecstasies; do not be surprised: kneel down and adore. You may even wither in the desert-lands of despair, just where God will be the closest to you: prostrate before him and adore again.

Necessary Precautions

CANONICAL TEXTS, apocryphal texts, and words attributed to our Master found scattered in religious works of the first centuries (*Agrapha*)[2] relate but a few of the multiple healings he performed. These writings do not even mention all those known to Christ's contemporaries. Moreover, they remain mute as to special means Jesus used at times.

To believe Jesus never used anything but prayer would be to minimize his power to a very small scale. Mere humans that we are, we should and can only use prayer. Seizure on our part of an immaterial force would constitute an usurpatory violence. Were we true Christians, we would not pick

---

[2] Sayings of Jesus that are not found in the canonical gospels.

Mystical Healings

a single fruit, would not swallow a morsel, would not begin any work whatsoever without first asking the Father's permission and protection, because all things belong to him alone, and from him alone do we receive all things. To omit taking care of this detail renders our works illegitimate.

But Jesus, being one with the Father—true form of the Father upon this world of relativities, Lord and Master of created beings—has legitimate command over all beings. He has that right. He need not render any account as to his purpose when he demands anything from them, since they hold their being and their life from him. Whatever his command may be, if they do not obey him, they are in the wrong. However, just as a respectful son (who, though well-qualified to tend and cultivate the family homestead on his own) does not do anything without first seeking his father's authorization, so too Jesus (who could make himself obeyed by the sea and mountain, by the devil and disease, by angels and men) never performs a miracle, never takes an initiative, without first seeking his celestial Father's consent—following which, he executes the works using the means he deems proper.

Should we not imitate Christ's deference down to our lowest tasks? As we offer a cup of broth to an ailing person, should we not ask the Father to please bless it, since we are totally ignorant of the spiritual virtues of this remedy—of the plant that furnished its substance, of the agents that may have modified the properties of its species, where it bloomed, and of the hands that handled it? Does not botanical chemistry teach us that plant essences are modified by the soil, the seasons, even the hours? Does not biological chemistry teach us that organisms produce different reactions according to the passions they are subjected to?

THE HEALINGS OF CHRIST

When in contact with a sick person, impatience will have a different physiological action than pity, humility a different one than complacency. How much more efficacious, then, could our care be after having called upon God for help? This rule applies still more rigorously to non-material therapeutics, the use of which demands still greater prudence.

The fact that we are able to perceive more clearly and completely those forms of universal life that chemistry, physics, and natural science are at work researching shows that our domain at the present time is the "world of bodies," that we can make use of its products, that we should improve it through our industry; and that then, through our efforts to attain holiness, we are meant to take that world along in our wake towards the world of the spirit. We have the right to search for all possible remedies in the three realms. We have the duty of making our discoveries known without avarice and to render to God the homage of gratefulness that rightfully belongs to him.

But we are insatiable. Not satisfied with exploiting the infinite resources of physical nature, even before we have exhausted it, because each of its three kingdoms (mineral, vegetable, animal) contains within itself remedies for all diseases), we recklessly venture into unknown realms. For instance, there is magnetism, a marvelous auxiliary, of course, but how pure should be the hands to administer it without peril! There is spiritualism, which disturbs our deceased and disequilibrates our mediums. There are the magic arts, which constrain invisible beings, imprison them, deport them, or kill them. There is brutal hypnotism. There are forms of suggestion that enchain instead of liberating, that provoke revolt instead of healing.

The most powerful magnetists, however, do not under-

Mystical Healings

stand magnetism any better than the ablest athletes understand neuro-muscular laws. All sorts of diseases resist the treatments of the learned doctors. No one can state with certitude just what spirits, elementals, and gods are, or how a suggestion differs from a hypnotic command, from a mental concentration, from an act of will. Doubtless, thousands of books speak of all these matters, but they cannot teach us the truth because their authors are not in the truth—that is, in the Word. I too am well aware that I also lack such comprehensive knowledge. But I have at least the advantage, as have you, of knowing that I know nothing. Because we are aware of our ignorance, we adhere to Christ alone. And so, from time to time, when the need arises, and owing to our weakness, Christ himself shows us the truth regarding such and such a point.

I am only giving you general facts, because no matter how prudent we have become, or how low we can sink into the consciousness of our nothingness, the temptation for knowledge remains always possible: a fall remains possible, and possession of a secret always entails a responsibility. For so long as we do not accomplish all of our duties in full (the family, social, and professional duties that our meager knowledge of the physical world engenders), God will not reveal any of the invisible mysteries to us—because we would not know how to use them without harming others or ourselves. Those disciples to whom the Word reveals a secret use it in order to help their brothers, but they do not share it otherwise, for fear some imprudent or vainglorious person would seize it.

Many a doctrine claiming to lead to the manipulation of unknown forces are being exhumed today. But they are all of them in error. The occult energies that esotericism stud-

THE HEALINGS OF CHRIST

ies are but created forces, which means they also are subject to the mechanical laws of relativity, laws whose action is limited and whose application requires precise conditions. Similarly to nature, these forces are only inverted reflections of other forces, of absolute, real, unconditioned forces belonging to the kingdom of God, to the world of glory whose chief is Jesus. These forces are the agents of Christ's miracles; their action is unfathomable and perfect; they lie beyond the reach of any who live without Christ. Moreover, even among those who work within the law of Christ, very few become so worthy as to receive one of them. Theology refers to them as the graces or gifts of the Holy Spirit.

There are never more than three servants of Christ on earth who are perfect enough to become instruments of these eternal forces. Yet not one of them equals the human perfection of Jesus. Moreover, even the most perfect of creatures remains infinitely distant from the divine splendor of Christ. Even the wisest do nothing but recite a lesson gathered by his immortal being. Even the most powerful thaumaturge, if he is a Christian, handles but a fire on loan from heaven. Or, if he is not a Christian, he handles but a fire purloined by ruse or by violence from the secret smithies of nature. Jesus alone appears omnipotent and omniscient. He alone teaches with authority. He alone commands without need of sanction.

Thus, humility, a constant and plenary humility, seems to be the first and necessary condition to heal in the name of God, a humility that contains the forgiving of all trespasses—and the forgetting of them too. The kind of humility that reduces our self-esteem to such a degree that our adversaries cannot find a single place to wound. The kind of humility that contains all obediences and all renouncements. The kind of humility that engenders confidence, inalterable joy, gentle peace, and that wafts the sweet fragrances of eternal gardens all about.

We do not really know how much everything rests upon the Father. Even the most venerated of his servants, as startling as their discourses may seem to us, have never seen how far-reaching or how deeply this universal dependence extends. The world lives from God. More tightly woven even than the untearable gossamer of the infinitely small, the web of providence envelops and penetrates us on all sides. As gigantic as he is, Satan himself and his formidable revolts only succeed in widening here and there some of the mesh of the living network of love. And as far as the revolts of human beings are concerned, they would be laughable were they not pitiable. It is not the awareness of our weakness that should make us good, but the recognition of our ingratitude. It is not our little acts that wound the paternal heart of God, but their principle of perversity.

The Genesis of Illness

A BINDING ENGAGEMENT of grave and tacit responsibility takes place at the moment when a disciple comes before a sick person. He stands there in the name of Christ, under his cover, employing the forces that his sufferings have created, taking his place, I dare say it. The earthly intelligence of the patient and of the onlookers may not be able to perceive this formidable substitution; but their spirits see it, the angels see it, and the invisible ones also see it. We risk, at any moment, a frightfully burdensome trust that demands superhuman perseverance and profound humility.

It was necessary to recall these things to mind before pur-

THE HEALINGS OF CHRIST

suing our study. For the tenderness of the Father hides his grandeur from us. Christ does likewise: because of the consuming desire he has to save us, he makes himself seem so similar to us that we forget both his power and his incomparable beauty. The inner gesture by which we, mere atoms before measureless Being, turn our spirit to God—yes, this very gesture, seen as it really is—should appear to us as the boldest of audacities, one we should not permit ourselves to have except when in the throes of sacred fear. But by dint of repeatedly hearing that God is good, that his indulgence is infinite, that his love grants us everything, we lose the respect we should have, and our associations with him become insolent familiarity.

Let us reactivate these elementary but indispensable notions within us from time to time.

The supreme prerogatives that our Lord Christ received from the Father are perpetually offered to us by him. It is up to us to receive them. For that, our spirit must enter into the palace where legions of angels guard them. The keys to this palace are forged by the works of fraternal love, the most simple and yet the most difficult of which are: abstaining from slander and defending the absent ones from such attacks. But merely paying an occasional visit to the marvelous palace does not suffice: we must make ourselves worthy to live in it, to live in it as if we had been born there, to take on its manners, its language, and its cast of mind. Hence, you must systematically apply your efforts to having great indulgence towards the faults of others, utmost rigor against your own faults, and discretion in language—these, plus a spontaneous zeal towards the weak, are the signs by which the hearts who dwell in the light are recognized.

Mystical Healings

Thousands of times you will have to repeat the same effort before your tongue refuses to pronounce one single unkind word; but later you will become friends of Christ, and citizens of heaven. Everything to be found therein—its fruits, springs, harmonies, energies, all eternal prototypes of the natural forces that positive science and occultism try to seize—you will be able to use. You will be able, in the name of Jesus, to have command over illness, tempests, death, and wild animals—all without training, restraints, formulas, or rites.

It is this kind of speech the Scriptures designate under the name of "gift of tongues." For instance, when the friend of God makes a speech in French (or any other language), the audience, no matter what country they are from, will understand him. If they question him in any kind of idiom, he will hear their question and they will understand his answer. Even animals, plants, and stones can communicate with the true disciple. Moreover, as everything in the universe of the spirit is bound together, possessing any one of its innumerable powers (there are more than seven) procures for the one who receives its benefits the sum-total of light that his being can absorb. But that is an entirely new subject.

In order to be able to heal others mystically, which means totally, healing the entire succession of the organs involved (from the spiritual center to the material body, from the ancestral origin of the disease down to its latest process of metastasis), the one who would heal must live a double life. One must see, hear, think, and act upon the earth, but as well, one must see the angels and immortal spirits, converse with them, work with them, contemplate celestial fields, and comprehend divine purposes. Such is the existence of the liberated one.

THE HEALINGS OF CHRIST

    Before reaching that state, we can only take care of the sick, help the unfortunate, and pray for one and all. Yes, that is all we can do; but then, these little things constitute a most rigorous duty. And when the fulfillment of these primary obligations mean expenses, labors, and disappointments, let us rejoice, because these burdens or annoyances, borne in love, will diminish the debt of our brothers. No matter how bitterly we have been deceived, no matter how unjustified it may seem to our short-sightedness, let us maintain a humble and robust faith. Still very far from the sublime function of the "soldier" who suffers as a holocaust, we languish in the debtor's prison: thus, no suffering can reach us unless it be just and bearable. What seems unjust and unbearable to us are the phantoms born out of our pride or out of our indolence.

    Never do our tribulations exceed our strength. Many a time, without our being aware of it, God, through the intermediary of one of his servants, postpones the balance-due of these debts, saves us from an illness, from an accident or a sorrow. Our very kind Father quite frequently uses the pretext of the little good we have done to cause the fatal trajectory of some suffering engendered by our faults in the past to swerve from our path. Furthermore, because of our efforts in doing our best, divine mercy gives us credit anyway for this unpaid debt.

    What can we conclude from all this? That a healing is always an unearned favor? All illicit processes that make use of magic or will-power do not cure, but merely keep the physical effects of the disease at bay, just as a thief cannot steal while he is incarcerated in a prison. Ordinary medicine heals the body. But, since it does not reach the spiritual (if the healed patient does not obtain the forgiveness of

Mystical Healings

his sin from heaven through perfect repentance and by living a better life), the disease can reappear at a later date with more virulence. If the cure comes as a result of prayer, the sick person is cleansed, unless it happens that he falls back into the sin that engendered the disease.

The sick person must in any case understand that he can regain health only if someone shoulders his debt. It is a fact that nothing once alive ever dies. Hence, the disease, when it leaves its victim, does not die. But the resignation of the sick, their courage to become well, their regret for their past sins, their faith in God, and their prayers progressively change the rigor of the morbid virus. And so, a pure disciple, a soldier of Christ, can, even through his voluntary holocaust, change this venom into balm, and this hell into a paradise. The human process can track down, diagnose, or lessen the disease, but only the mystical process can transform or regenerate it.

However, no one (and the soldier of Christ no more than the common faithful) has the right to take the illness of another upon himself voluntarily, because no one is the master of his body. Of course, it is understood that all operations of substitution—of grafting upon a tree or into an animal, and all magic enchainments—are forbidden by heaven. These are crimes, and it would apply quite appropriately to state in their case "that the remedy is worse than the disease." The free-man who heals the sick pays for the other—but in this case it is through a transposition of merits, through a spiritual clearing. By contrast, when a doctor heals the sick by natural therapeutic means, there also occurs a displacement of debts, although now entirely different from the previous one: the remedy gives a "shot in the arm" or surplus of energy to the organism, and the effort it makes to defend itself brings to it the gratuitous help of divine mercy. But here it is only the body that has been helped—the spiritual sin or "blemish" still subsists, because a free-man alone can remove it, and by thus eradicating it produce a complete cure. The time has not yet come to understand all the phenomena regarding this mechanism in detail. Better for us to pray, whether we are the sick, the doctors, or simple servants of Christ.

Someday we will possess the Holy Spirit: I mean, the Holy Spirit will possess us, and will accomplish through our intermediation all that which men are attempting to do through their personal will, through their brain, or through magnetism. No being resists the commands of the Spirit, the stone on the path no more than the suns of the milky way—whatever the momentary circumstances might be. The innumerable and instantaneous healings of Christ bear the seal of the Spirit. Let us never forget that this sovereign power exercised by free-men carries with it the painful counterpart I have just mentioned to you: the inner and perpetual martyrdom of love. The Spirit is love, and he hovers only upon hearts in which nothing else but love exists. Let us not be foolhardy; let us not attempt to imitate these exceptional lives. Let us be content with bringing solace to our brothers through all the little means that lie within our power—because never failing to make one of these modest efforts is already a difficult task.

Diseases

DISEASES ARE the painful results of undecipherable mysteries. Only those who have become incapable of being impatient towards the exigencies of the sick (even when

Mystical Healings

they seem unjustified) as well as incapable of condemning their neighbor (even if he seems responsible for his miseries) can penetrate the primary causes and the spiritual causes of disease. If these causes were unveiled to us (we who are vain, aggressive, and jealous of our comforts), we would use them as pretexts to get rid of those who suffer. We would show ourselves so hard, so pitiless, towards these bothersome people that we would draw cruel destiny down upon us. Then, the same obstacles, the same enemies that caused our brothers to fall, would make us fall much faster and lower than they, because of our pride. The number of sick would increase, and new diseases would be born—as happens during the epochs of Judgment. The ignorance in which heaven keeps us is therefore prudent and kind.

For instance, if we happen to see some poor man fall on the sidewalk in a fit, and we inwardly think: "So what: it's his fault, he didn't have to take a drink, did he?"—at that very moment we change the course of our destiny: our being is drawn towards a set of circumstances such that sooner or later we will be faced with the same problems or the same weaknesses that have made of this man an alcoholic. Will we be able to withstand these problems any better than he did? Probably not, because we will have placed too much confidence in our own strength.

On the other hand, if in face of this same spectacle we abstain from giving in to the scorn we feel rising within us only because we fear having to face a similar temptation later, we are not being charitable, but cleverly selfish. And so in this case, on some "rainy day," destiny will doubtless place us in the grips of someone else's calculating selfishness.

If, however, we regard this poor wretched being rolling in

THE HEALINGS OF CHRIST

the dirt rather as a body torn by suffering, as a spirit overcome by sorrow, and we try to calm and comfort both, then perhaps—because we have refused to see the darkness where our poor brother was groaning—God might stir the light lying dormant in the bottom of his heart, and this poor wretch will be healed. To obtain such miracles, all that is needed is love—fraternal, efficacious love, devoid of calculations, of hesitations, of regrets.

What can be done so as not to judge? Everyone knows that a particular disease originates through a certain vice. Yes, that is surely true. But what we must not say is: "I, I did not fall into such a trap, and I shall not fall into it." On the contrary, one must accept the fact that one can easily fall into it, because it is quite evident that all the members of the human family carry within themselves the seeds of all ills and of all good, and that it is always the greater before God who believe themselves the least. No one can condemn another, especially as providence knows perfectly well how to extract good out of evil.

We are consumed with the thirst for knowledge, but to quench it we venture in search of adventure instead of waiting for God to teach us whatever he thinks we are ready for. A while back, I gave you an example of the difficult situations we get entangled in because of our impatience. Yet the efforts we make to extricate ourselves, no matter how awkward they may be, develop our forces, and we advance even though we lose our way occasionally. Gentle, kind, divine solicitude makes use of our errors for our progress.

Hence, dear disciples of Jesus, to heal the sick we must confine ourselves to prayers, meanwhile alleviating their pain through our charity. The observance of the teachings of the gospels constitutes the sole method and the sole

Mystical Healings

training our Master offers us, that we may someday emulate his miracles. When he healed, to some he said "Thy faith has made thee whole" and to the others "Thy sins are forgiven thee." But as for us, we have no right of demanding faith or of discovery of the sins of those we want to help. All we can do is to ask for them, with them, or in their stead, that divine mercy will save them, and do so by reinforcing our request by some kind of sacrifice, or by a spiritual fast. Especially, let us not forget that many people suffer for causes other than their own personal expiation. However, there are such strange cases that might sometimes come your way, that certain notions can be useful for keeping intact your confidence in divine kindness, in divine justice, and your certitude that the Father sees everything and that nothing happens without his permission.

There are, in the human being, two spiritual hearths or centers whose flames burn in opposite directions, because they are of opposite nature. One is natural life (the self, selfishness, the body and its instincts); the other is supernatural life (pure love, the spirit and its aspirations). What the one rejects, the other seeks. The happiness of one means pain to the other. Also, one of the goals of existence is to reunite these divergent flames, to make the spirit descend into the body, to make the corporeal body ascend to the level of spiritual life—to blend them, unite them, and have them live harmoniously.

Our self, our free-will that is still in swaddling clothes, hesitates between these pulls. Rarely is it able to discern whether it is the body or the spirit that gives vent to the moans that trouble the self. As it is closest to the body, the self will often favor the body—it will not accede easily to the wishes of the spirit. Instead, it will put all the resources of nature into gear so as to heal this body, searching even into the forbidden regions for more powerful means of cure. Prayer and moral purification alone can save that self which favors the body from the dual error of revolt against suffering and use of illicit means (illicit, because dangerous).

This is the origin of the constant battle whose theater of conflict is our personality. Before birth, our self (which exists already) is informed by certain angels of the work it must accomplish during the earthly existence it is being given. In certain rather rare cases, it can choose among several types of labor, but this choice is only offered if the light within the self is strong enough to give it the courage to choose the most arduous career—the one offering the means for its greatest purification. For the great majority of births, on the contrary, no choice is proposed: the subject only perceives the expected tests. But as he finds himself at that moment within the light (which his angel-guides brought in their wake), he sees things from the standpoint of heaven; he judges himself at his true value, and generally accepts in advance the trials unfolded before him.

When an incurable invalid moans and rebels on his bed of pain, it is the body that resists, while the luminous spirit of this martyr may very well be rejoicing in the exaltation of this accepted sacrifice. The recumbent body before you is unaware of this profound drama. Inversely, the spirits of the strong, the lucky ones whom we see triumphant and profiting in life, do in truth suffer and lament in the mortal shadows that the joys of the world represent. Thus, let us never judge. Let us never will for our sick to be healed. Our prayers, which are humbly said, must never turn into willful commands to the illness. That is an all too slippery slope!

Mystical Healings

False Healings

ARE THERE PROCESSES of combating suffering that heaven does not want us to employ? Does heaven demand that we suffer? My answer is "yes" to the first question and "no" to the second. The Father, Christ, the Virgin, and all inhabitants of heaven suffer when they witness our suffering. They suffer when the least of creatures suffers. Therefore, they give us the means to avoid suffering, means that are efficacious and without risks. And if certain immaterial remedies are forbidden us, it is because, after a temporary alleviation, these remedies would bring us a far greater and more irreducible illness or hardship.

As you know, there are numberless modes of life in the universe. We are only conscious of a few in the physical, the mental, and affective states. But there exist still other physical spheres, other intellectual spheres, and many other ways of loving than those we know. The consciousness or awareness man has of one of these modes of life in general is the sign that he is permitted to make use of that mode. It is a garden into which he enters at a precise stage of his evolution. He must cultivate that field, and has the right of picking the plants, the fruits, and the flowers he has helped grow. But he does not have the right to trespass into another garden, either by force or by ruse, so as to pick its fruits, which might prove poisonous for him—and in any case, the watchmen will inevitably beat back the trespassing thieves.

In short, we have the right of using all that the mineral, plant, and animal kingdoms offer us to heal our bodies. It is our duty. But to take the spirit of a plant or of an animal for a transplantation, as per Paracelsus; to attach a disease to a stone or to a tree, as do sorcerers; to drive the disease away by means of elementary spirits, as the magicians teach; to give an order to the disease in our own name, following the method used by practitioners of "suggestion"—these are all forbidden by heaven. They weigh down a being innocent of that disease, they infringe upon the liberty of a creature, they disarrange what providence has organized, and they make of man a god of pride instead of the humble servant he should be to others. Finally, these methods heal only for a time; and as stated in the gospel parable, the illness driven away thus returns with seven companions, and the state of the patient worsens. Happy is the foolhardy healer who pays for his imprudence right now in this life, rather than in the next.

But the methods permitted, such as ordinary medical treatment, magnetism, and the intercession of saints, do not heal totally. Yes, they may cause the physical disease to disappear for a shorter or longer period of time, but they do not reach its spiritual cause. One cannot elevate the morals of a thief or of a drunkard by incarcerating them, because as soon as the prison door opens, and the bottle is once more to hand, each will continue from where he left off. Penalization does not change hearts. For the same reason, medical treatment affects only the body, and magnetic treatment affects only the etheric envelope. Moreover, the saint whom we invoke cannot change our soul either, because the faithful does not say: "Great saint, ask God to heal me!" but he says: "Great saint, heal me!"

The most frequent cause for the majority of diseases is sin: the spiritual heart has been vitiated, its corruption has spread throughout the diverse subtle bodies of man till it finally reaches his physical body. For a healing to be total and lasting, either the sick person must bear the test to the

Mystical Healings

end without complaints, with repentance, and with joy; or else an envoy of God must discover the original causal sin, and cleanse the spirit of the sick person just as Christ did; or else, a prayer must be said, either by the sick person or someone else—a prayer humble enough to reach divine mercy. Then God himself heals, by sending an angel.

Let us, for a moment, look closely at the last hypothesis, which is the one we are particularly interested in when we visit the sick.

To be able to heal, to transmute a morbid force into a health-giving force, one must have the faculty of piercing down into the very depths of hearts. One must have pure hands, worthy of pouring upon the blemishes of a conscience water from the eternal springs.

Love for one's fellow man, alone, procures us this privilege. This does not mean that love obtains it for us. It merely enables us to receive it. And it still has to be a love devoid of any kind of selfishness. Our charities must really be charitable acts; in other words, be gratuitous favors. For instance, when I meet a needy person, moved by spontaneous compassion, I may do everything in my power to be useful. But this gesture may be one in payment of a spiritual debt contracted once upon a time towards that person. So in the eyes of the just Judge, my charity is but payment of an account due—hence, an act of justice. Therefore, it cannot operate upon the spirit of that wretched person the remission of his sins. Moreover, if perchance my destiny has never been linked with his and I owe him nothing, then my charitable gesture is gratuitous; but, were he indebted to me, then the sacrifice I am making for him will give added power to my prayer, and heaven may grant to me the true healing of his suffering. This gift is rarely seen and almost always occurs in the case of a soldier of heaven who has re-descended here-below to accomplish a mission. So do try to follow that example *ad infinitum*, and you will be able to perceive Christ, who taught with authority, and who had command over devils without ever raising his voice.

The Devil and Disease

THE EVANGELISTS often cite the cure of people who were possessed of the devil. And so, because of that, modern commentators claim generally that those healed by Christ were but high-strung people, hysterics, or those prone to auto-suggestion. This is a biased and partial viewpoint. In the East today there still persists the belief in evil spirits that persecute man, and in elementary spirits, animators of all beings and of all physical phenomena. The Church has employed the resources of its doctrines and its discipline to extirpate this opinion. By so doing it has acted as a wise mother, because such theories open the gate to extravagant dreams and to the practice of superstitions. However, theologians do affirm the existence of invisible beings—angels, mixed spirits, and demons—and their constant participation in the movements of the visible world. This belief conforms with reality.

Were we circumspect and wise; were our knowledge of the hidden marvels of nature to have the unique effect of precipitating us before their supreme Lord in adoration; were the tiniest part of the influence we exert over nature only to increase our gratitude and humility; were the prerogatives heaven confers upon our human status to be used only for our brothers—then this mysterious nature would

Mystical Healings

have no more secrets from us, and would permit our drawing from its treasures unconditionally.

But we are not that wise. That is why our powerlessness to meddle with occult forces is a safeguard against our imprudence. In any case, we do not need these forces. If we but do our utmost to serve God and our fellowman wholeheartedly, we receive infinitely more precious and powerful forces from heaven.

Why should we launch into these uncertain and dangerous expeditions to probe the nature of demons, of elementals, and of spirits, instead of extirpating what lies within our reach—by which I mean the evil within ourselves? In school, a child's first lesson is not that of rhetoric; so let us start by first understanding what our immediate duty is, and then how to handle this instrument that is ourself. Let us analyze the evil hidden within us. When we have faced ourselves squarely and brought out all our darknesses into blazing light, then other fields will open to our inquiring eyes.

In the gospel, we note that evil spirits recognize the sovereign light of Jesus. Now, among beings, before cumulative rational knowledge comes, there always first exists an intuitive and immediate knowledge, the awareness of which remains more or less obscure because of the corporeal dross that sheathes our spiritual organism. Contemporary philosophy attempts to bring the mechanism of the unconscious to light. Little by little, philosophy discovers that the brain is not indispensable to thought, and that even knowledge can be produced by processes entirely different from sense perception or intellectual abstraction. In fact, one is apt to forget that the paraphernalia of the telegraphic system are not the electric current; that the nerves and the encephalon

THE HEALINGS OF CHRIST

are the apparatus that life sets into motion; that cerebration is the mental mechanism suited to the earth and to our present form of intelligence. But this intelligence, in itself, is one of the attributes of life. And two creatures—by the very fact that they are alive—may also understand each other with the facility proportionate to their freedom from the physical form that clothes them.

The earthly person of Christ veiled the splendor of his spiritual person. The witnesses to his works could understand the sublimity of his spiritual person only to the degree that they lived in the light. But the spirits, both good and evil, perceived this invisible splendor shining upon their kingdom much better, though they were less able to see the absolute splendor of the quality of the Son of God than could the disciples, in the heart of whom a spark of eternity, a particle of the redeeming Word, was already scintillating. Thus, demons know that they are dealing with the saint of God, but most of them ignore who this saint is in essence.

Why has God created evil spirits? Why is there suffering, why evil? And to top it all, why even is there Creation? Human intelligence cannot give a satisfactory answer to any of this, because it cannot see the other side of these problems: no one can be a common soldier and a generalissimo at the same time. Thus, in the religious order, there are a number of insoluble enigmas—insoluble because they are situated far beyond our psychological consciousness. And if, when confronted by them, we were to stop our search by an act of faith and humility, this act would pierce through to us someday as intuition (a contact with inexplicable and faraway reality), and we would then understand: the life within us would communicate with the life outside of us.

How closely we should heed the murmurs and the trem-

Mystical Healings

ors that the approach of creatures provoke in our hearts! Sensations of sympathy or antipathy, of fright or confidence, no matter how simple they seem, could give us an inkling whether the being who provokes them belongs to the light or to the darkness. Meeting a saint is more profitable than reading his books, because each book is but a refraction of his life. Meeting him gives power to the good there is in us and ameliorates the evil that also lurks therein. Our perfection is important only because it leads to the perfection of many other beings who are bound to us. In the spiritual world, we occupy a center post; we are pivots; we draw along with us, either upward or downward, to the right or to the left, a host of subordinate creatures. It is through us that demons can become benefic; it is through us that the radiation of angels can touch corporeal objects.

In attributing diseases to the action of evil spirits, the ancients were not entirely wrong. Sin, which is the primary cause of pathological disorder, binds to our spirit an agent of evil which, in turn, becomes its secondary cause; and the action of this agent upon our etheric organism brings about the functional alterations that are observed by medical science. Whether the trouble be of psychic or organic origin, Jesus, when he heals, always drives away the genii of this particular trouble. For instance, since the genii attacked the sick person only because immanent justice had given him the right to do so, when the thaumaturgist takes away his prey, he owes the genii some compensation: the sick must be purified of his spiritual illness, and the genii must be given a new means of living. To truly heal, one must be able to act upon the central plane of the invisible, where the essential archetypes of creatures and things exist under the immediate eye of the Word.

THE HEALINGS OF CHRIST

Conditions of Mystical Healing

THE JEWISH SCRIBES, in conformity with their doctrine, were well aware and recognized that God alone heals by his forgiveness of sins. To deny this axiom would have been heresy. But they did not have the courage to follow the logic of this dogma any further, which means to say that the man who heals by the forgiveness of sin has to be the Son of God and God himself; otherwise, he irresistibly draws to himself the thunderbolts of the Spirit. The scribes did not want Jesus to be that Son. The idolatry they had for their texts and their caste prejudices extinguished the light within them. Of course, to seek education is our duty. But intelligence, though an admirable instrument, can become dangerous if not kept under control, where it belongs. Knowledge acquired by study or observation is only a distant cousin of the school of living knowledge; it is a slow progress towards the world of the actual spiritual presences, where gardens no longer have fences, and the inhabitants have no secrets. The law orders that we cultivate our energies—whether they belong to our body, soul, or mentality—with the same effervescent solicitude, because no matter how weak, awkward, or shallow they might temporarily be, they are nonetheless germs of future powers whose breadth and vigor would overwhelm us, were we able to conceive of them today. In order to remain within our present horizon, just as the luxuriant forest is issued from some miserable beech sapling lost once upon a time in the mud, so the splendors of the great intellects who lead humanity are nothing but the rudimentary seedlings from rich organisms, the scintillating centers out of which someday our cerebral mechanism will be constituted.

Mystical Healings

Only a perfect man could endure the force and penetration of the most active and magnificent intellectual power that Jesus, the incarnate Word, possessed. Just as the common soldier can only fathom two or three out of a hundred reasons that have inspired the orders of a general, neither can our brain understand or fathom in its profoundest search but the thousandth part of the true perspectives that Jesus's intellect could perceive at a single glance. So, we do not, and never really will, understand him. Even our greatest intellects, when studying the gospel, can only compress its perspectives to their own level, or amputate its broader radiations. The acts of Christ seem to us as being unrelated, contradictory, and illogical. And if perchance the exegetes do find some kind of order therein, even an arbitrary one, it is due to the simplification and the effort of their rationalism—i.e., it is because they ignore or deny the existence of the innumerable invisible threads by which beings are connected to each other throughout space and in all modes of time.

When Jesus looked at a man, at an animal, at a tree, a creature, a hill, a character, even a house—in one glance he saw all the being's previous ancestry, present relationships, and future descendents. Hence, there were all sorts of reasons why he did not act towards that being as we might have done. For instance, he calls the multitudes; he comes to them; then he shies away from them and orders them not to speak; he hides on the mountaintops; he draws the attention of his most powerful enemies, and then he disappears as if frightened; he, the pacifier, speaks of war, of conflagrations, and even gestures with violence; he, the all-powerful, trembles; he, the meek, calls people down, using virulent terms. How can we reconcile these contradictions?

THE HEALINGS OF CHRIST

First of all, let us understand that they are not contradictions. Let us remember that divine beings live inversely from reasonable human beings, since the whole of nature is the inverted image of the eternal kingdom. The leaders among men think they should seek the limelight, take the best seats in the front row, be seen by all—either because they think they can be more useful to the crowd by climbing upon a pedestal, or because they have an exalted opinion of themselves. The servants of heaven, on the contrary, hide themselves. They seek anonymity, accepting to live in the obscurity that ignorance, hatred, or ingratitude allots them, because it is in the outer darkness that the inner light shines most brilliantly. And yet, it is essential that the light also shine before the vainglories of political power, social wealth, and rational knowledge, so that on Judgment Day the false gods cannot claim not having ever seen truth.

Hence, if the ways of the Spirit are inscrutable, our attitude must remain one of humility—not only before his ways, but before everything, since without scrutiny we are not yet able to discern from all that comes our way whether it is brought to us by the Spirit of God or by the spirit of this world. Let us anchor humility deep within our whole being. Let us anchor humility in our heart by repentance, by a tested repentance, through the reparations of our fraudulent dealings against our brothers. Because if one has stolen, before he can be healed, before heaven may grant the healing, before it can heal him, not only must he repay the capital, but as well the accumulated interests of that theft. No casuistry will ever lessen this requisite. Also, there must be humility of the heart, acquired by being conscious of all the wrong one has done, and all the good one has failed to do. "I have never harmed anyone!" exclaims the

Mystical Healings

impatient sick person. Alas, what a reckless word! It instantly stops divine mercy and prevents divine aid from helping him. Also, there must be humility in one's opinions. How often the sick complain of the indifference of their doctors, and of their ignorance! They accuse them of cupidity and hardheartedness. But... we only seemingly choose our doctor. We have the doctor we deserve to have. By passing judgment upon him we prevent heaven from inspiring him. By refusing the prayers offered us, whatever they might be, we also prevent heaven from acting in our behalf. There must be humility in our self-pride: through forgiveness, through forgetting any trespasses against us. A sick person who asks for heaven's help, but who at the same time does not stop his lawsuit, who does not throw the IOUs and promissory notes from his unfortunate insolvent debtors into the fire, may be helped temporarily through medical science, but heaven will not save him—neither him nor those he loves. We must also have the humility to bear physical torment, because, no matter how repugnant our disease, it is the one we have merited and that will purify our heart best. Moreover, it is not haphazardly that the Church says, along with us: "Lord, save us from sudden death!" A long illness is a wonderful illness: one has the time to see one's limitations, and time to repent and pray. Remorse is the cauterizing effect of light upon our invisible ulcers. We must not shy away from this red-hot iron; on the contrary, we must accept it, ask for it, submit to it—and joyously. In this way we save ourselves from many misfortunes in after-death. We must also have humility when choosing remedies, and overcome impatience during a long illness; for the money we pay the doctor, the pharmacist, and the surgeon is part of force and life that circulates and

THE HEALINGS OF CHRIST

carries away our ills little by little. It is better to live impoverished than to die rich. People ask: "In this case, why do so many poor die in misery after living a life of martyrdom?" My answer is: "For many reasons. I know a few, but I dare not let you know them, because we could not stop ourselves from passing judgment upon each sick person, and we would draw frightful consequences upon ourselves." The law presiding at the genesis of illnesses is a simple one. Luckily, we are ignorant of it, because otherwise we would condemn our brothers. And then another law—the whiplash type of law, or spiritual reaction—would inexorably set in. For instance, a patient tortured by cancer wants his dressing changed several times a day. This may irritate us; we say so; and we tell everyone around us that we are sick and tired of it all: this alone is sufficient to place us someday on the path of cancer so that we may experience the resignation that a cancerous patient has to exert so as not to be a drain upon those who surround him. Finally, we have to have humility even in the body and in the vital spirit of our organs. For the healing to take place medically, the sick organ must desire the remedy; but, especially for any healing to be true and become final, the sick organ, welcoming grace and light, must repent, resign itself, and even forget its illness, just as our heart forgets its sorrows in the beatitude of faith.

So, the possibility of our corporeal salvation resides in our heart. This heart must be hewn, carved, and forged so as to become the tabernacle of light. Sufferings of all kinds are the necessary handmaidens for this work, and we cannot escape them, no matter what ruse we may seek to employ. By rejecting them, we only make our work that much harder: it is far better for us to accept immediately

Mystical Healings

and willingly. In any event, heaven needs our goodwill—how rarely do we ever see Jesus change a perverse heart! It is because, in order to be viable, our mystical orientation has to proceed from free-will, that we cannot achieve anything in this domain except through our own will. God awaits us, he does not take us in spite of ourself.

Since we are athirst for heaven, in order to be healed we must, besides that thirst, also have a fund of merits to our credit, thanks to which the cessation of our trials may be compensated. These are: zeal and self-sacrifice; refraining from slander; having a living remembrance of Jesus (who two thousand years ago no doubt healed other people who were suffering from the same disease). Or else, counter-balancing what a disease would have meant to us, we accept a new work instead—such as adopting children, forgiving debts, dropping a lawsuit, doing good work. These are the means by which help arrives, and our spirit is removed from the path of the disease and placed upon the path of the healing angels. Also, it may happen that another being takes our load upon his shoulders: someone we know; a soldier of heaven who is passing by; someone from afar whom we do not know; perhaps an animal; perhaps even our dog. Do not be amazed, everything is possible: we are ignorant of so many things!

Human methods soothe; yes, they drive away and weaken the disease, but they do not heal permanently, because even after death the disease can continue. In order to be of benefit, medication should always be prepared with the help of prayer and by taking definite precautions. Remedies that come from the mineral kingdom are best when prepared in subterranean laboratories where we are certain they will not receive either the rays of the sun or of the moon. Those remedies that come from either the plant or animal kingdoms should be gathered before sunrise, and also with a prayer. As far as surgery is concerned, it keeps us from dying, of course, but it does not heal, since it has only a physiological effect. However, if the patient endures the operation with perfect resignation and courage, it is possible that heaven will be sufficiently satisfied with this resignation to erase his sin. But the surgical intervention has nothing to do with this mystical consequence. Let us mention in passing that we should always remember that everything is alive, that the amputated member continues to live, though to a lessened degree. It continues to be connected to the body to which it belonged, and this link subsists until the end of time. It is this member that, in fact, on the day of the Last Judgment, will permit the resurrection of the flesh. One should carefully bury such amputated parts, placing them in the safekeeping of the soil, so as to protect them from any ulterior injury. Heaven does not authorize the use of hypnotism—because it commands. Heaven permits magnetism, provided it is practiced with prayer and with totally pure hands. This last condition may be exceedingly difficult to fulfill, because all of us men and women, no matter how loyal or dedicated has been our life, have to meet temptation—for Christ has said that even the most fleeting thought, should we stop to heed it for but an instant, equals the act. Let us, then, accustom ourselves to be meticulous in all our dealings with others. Using such precautionary measures, magnetism becomes a marvelous auxiliary; it permits operating upon people from a distance, even upon people unknown to us. I will not give any further explanations, given that pride is ever curious about mysteries: it is useless to feed them to pride, since it would corrupt them.

Mystical Healings

Finally, as we mentioned previously, the finest method used for healing is simple prayer. All we need do is mention the name of the sick person to God, and say: "Heal him, if such is thy will." It is needless to strain our mind, to try to find out where the evil came from, to try to visualize the person who is absent, to feel the curative forces passing through us. We must not try any of this, but rest content that we shall experience it if it is God's will. On the other hand, what has to be done is to live according to the gospel faithfully, ardently, with all our might. It is not so much the intensity of a prayer that matters as its preparation. If we spend one quarter of an hour each day repeating the list of names of the sick we know, we must first of all spend the remaining twenty-three hours and forty-five minutes living according to heaven's standards, living as perfect disciples. Thus will our spirit be closer to Jesus, and it will be quite sufficient for us to express our desires to him plainly, simply, and without seeking to experience any extraordinary sensations.

Such requests are immediately transmitted through angelic armies from one hierarchy to another. It is exceedingly rare that the Word hears them directly, although it is to him alone, or to the Virgin, that we should address our prayers, and not to his angels or to his saints. It is through the merits of the Only Son and of the One Mother that we may intercede with the Father. You do understand now, I hope, that in order to heal in the name of God (at least, until such time as we can read upon the forehead of the sick and in his heart the whole genesis of his illness, even from before his birth, and our mouth may say to him, "Go, thy sins are forgiven thee"), it is not power or intelligence that are needed, but selflessness, humility, and prudence. Evil trembles and departs in face of one who thinks himself nothing. These words are inscribed in the light. For the present, the rule to follow is for man to employ all the legitimate means that art and nature offer him, because medical science has to reach its relative state of perfection—and also man has to learn to depend upon God alone, because someday medicine will have to disappear before the instantaneous miracles of the Spirit.

Why need we live in anxiety? We are the children of a just and munificent Father. When suffering comes our way, it means that the Father wants our good, because only suffering can spiritualize us, because it is during times of great adversities that great miraculous help comes—only, let us not obstruct their road through our pusillanimity.

Humility

THERE ARE CERTAIN questions in collective hygiene that we have to take under consideration, such as vaccines. We must conform to civilian and military regulations, although recognizing that if our destiny is to succumb, no serum will protect us from typhoid or smallpox; that if it is God's will, we will be able to go through epidemics and come into contact with contagious diseases without risk, without being vaccinated. Let us remain humble, in any case; let us not bargain with God. The one who shies away from a troublesome injection for himself or his child, believing that heaven will definitely protect him, is in error. The one who treats cholera patients without having taken the necessary preventative injections must not believe that heaven will make him immune. If heaven deems it good for him to die while performing his duty, this will be a worthy

Mystical Healings

death (his past and his future will be assuaged from it). If on the other hand heaven protects him from being contaminated, this will still be a grace (since we are unnecessary servants).

When leaving a contagious patient, we must see that our hands and clothing are aseptic. If we do not fear the contagion for ourself, well and good, but we do not have the right make anyone else run the risk by carrying upon ourself the pathogens. Also, if we happen to be infected with an infectious disease, we do not have the right of contaminating those who come close to us. We should be careful and use all available means to see that soiled linen, the expectorant vessels and cups we use, are out of their reach, because we will be held responsible for the accidents resulting from our negligence. We are responsible for the consequences of a sprained ankle resulting from the orange peel we discarded, or of the conflagration caused by the lighted match we flicked away.

Generally speaking, each person must undergo all forms of suffering. This is so, because our heart is hard, and unless we have experienced the pains of our brothers, we do not understand them, nor do we feel compassion for them. So, whenever we have a choice between running a risk or avoiding it, the first is the better and purer choice, because it implies strong reliance upon God. Furthermore, since we must love our neighbor as ourselves, we must remember that if we shoulder that accident, it will not strike our brother. Thus it is that we follow the school of divine love by suffering in the stead of another. I know that such things are difficult for ordinary wisdom to accept. See it only as an indication towards perfection, and good only for those who have definitively dedicated themselves to the service of heaven in profound humility and with the kind of courage that tribulations exalt rather than crush.

Disturbances in the interconnections between the spiritual man, the fluidic man, and the physical man can engender grave pathological disorders such as apoplexy, epilepsy, and most mental illnesses. For this reason, do not force a child who is afraid of the dark to sleep without a nightlamp; the child may feel and see a presence we adults do not anymore perceive (there are semi-material forms that a light keeps away; nocturnal frights may cause nervous convulsions and even tumors in a child). Do not awaken suddenly anyone who is peacefully asleep, or any somnambulistic subject. Neither should we recall to reality any individual deeply immersed in thought. Cases of sudden death are numerous enough, without multiplying them through imprudent acts. Aneurisms have physiological causes that doctors are aware of—but of which I say that they also have hyperphysical causes. If the spirit of a man wandering through inner spheres is suddenly recalled brutally into the body, there occurs an inflow of blood into the brain, into the cerebellum, or into the heart—to the violence of which the blood vessels must resist, otherwise death would ensue.

Neither must we focus our thoughts upon another person's thoughts in the hope of influencing him, even if we do it with an honest intention. Why? Because our thought, wandering through space in search of the other thought, may have to withstand the attacks of hostile beings, or may pick up morbid germs while adventuring through odious regions. It might even lose its way, or incite fright in the individual it visits; or, without meaning to, it may bring an illness to the person it visits, or bring one back to our body upon its return. It may also cause the spirit of the person

Mystical Healings

sought to come out, and the person becomes insane; or else, certain beings, taking advantage of our being "absent," might move into our person, and it is we who then become insane. Indeed, the diverse forms of mental alienation usually originate in a crisis of the unconscious. A human spirit out of its body can enter (whether we will or no) into another body. A human spirit who has wanted to subjugate another will probably be condemned by Justice to become in turn the slave of some invisible tyrant. A human spirit that obstinately seeks to uncover some forbidden mystery loses control and disorganizes its brain—these are the multiple reasons why the causes of insanity escape the psychiatrist. There are still many wicked actions that bind our organs, and that even the skill of a physician cannot discover: a tumor, a malformation, local paralysis, and rheumatism may sometimes be nothing but the physiological sign of a partial possession.

I will end these brief indications by reminding you once more that I offer them only as examples of the complexity of vital phenomena and of the gravity of our acts. The whole unknown that we discover at each step we take should cause humble sentiments of our ignorance and awareness of our responsibilities to be born in our heart. But let us never make use of the glimpse heaven permits us to have to try to find out the primary cause of a disease, or to judge our brothers. Let us, rather, use it to lessen our own selfishness, our pride, and our laziness. We must become indulgent towards others; and towards ourselves we must remain rigorous.

It is indispensable for the one who prays for others to be humble, severe towards himself, and feel gentleness for others; and to have prudence, also.

THE HEALINGS OF CHRIST

To heal mystically, no other knowledge is necessary than comprehension of one's own nothingness. No other energy is necessary than the force to thwart the self. One must maintain under perpetual surveillance the oh-so-clever, lively, stubborn self-will that is so often hidden within our purest desires. It is truly the hundred-headed hydra: when enchained on one side, it rears up on the other side; annihilated through a gesture of great abnegation, here it pops out again a few minutes or a few weeks later. It is of course man's great moral transmutation that is the most formidable enterprise there is. Let us be aware that the more we advance, the greater our difficulties, and the more helping aid abounds. This triple harmonious development gives rise to the birth of the "free-man"—the perfect being whom the Holy Spirit constructs by combining with his regenerating breath our person, the tempters who were converted by us, and our collaborators of all kinds.

Humility is so indispensable a quality for spiritual relations between man and heaven that God often prevents his servants from discovering certain facts, knowledge of which would be susceptible of awakening within them certain feelings of glorification too difficult to overcome. This was the condition of the apostles, who, all during their earthly existence, ignored the dignity of their spiritual origin. Today, in some organizations of initiates, one meets numerous so-called reincarnations of celebrated people: so many a Joan of Arc, a Mary Magdalene, a Virgin Mary, a Napoleon, a Charlemagne, and others! We must not make fun of such candor. We are unaware of all the secrets of the unconscious, and, in fact, very few among us are above some sort of ridiculous vanity. What is important is to forewarn the good faith of the searcher. No envoy of God knows his par-

Mystical Healings

ticular spiritual identity. The moment a man claims to be the reincarnation of an apostle, for instance, that means he suffers from hallucinations, or is an impostor. Let us assiduously apply ourselves to remaining humble; let us remember that Judas was the most advanced of the apostles, and that he fell because of his pride.

Now we can understand why (as the gospel stories tell), right after speaking of his healings, the right-thinking Jews were surprised to see Jesus among the poor, and his disciples living in joy—and just what, at this point of the story, the parable of the piece of new cloth and new wine means.

There are other diseases beside those stemming from physiological disorders. Ignorance is a disease; coarseness is a disease; prejudices are diseases as dangerous as cancer or tuberculosis; and as the mere presence of Jesus could calm the disturbances of the body, his glance and voice could also dissipate the vices due to intellect or habits. We are aware every day of the joy our bodies experience in being filled with the sun and pure air; this perfect sun who is Christ beatifies our total being a great deal more. His law is not one of rigor or penance, it is one of benevolence and deliverance; it drives all clouds away, breaks all chains, overcomes all weariness, and gives us rest. We who hope to be disciples should stand close enough to the Master to bathe in his peaceful radiation, so that his sovereign joy illuminates our faces and radiates upon our brothers the happiness of eternal certitudes.

But the piece of new cloth tears the old cloth apart, and the new wine pierces the worn-out goat-skin. This is what the non-Christian masters of spiritual life do. They cannot renovate the entire personality of their disciples; they sew, here and there, according to their power; they patch up, they pour too strong a draught into an inflexible mind, or into a worn-out sensitivity. Jesus alone, who knows us throughout, can regenerate us from the bottom up. So, when souls come to you, be prudent; help them more by your example than by your preaching; by the sacrifices you make secretly rather than by your criticisms; by your prayers more than by your lectures. Christ alone can give us the old wine of eternal wisdom; temporal wisdom can only give us new wines.

    This parable makes allusion to the excesses of power of which certain initiates are guilty, especially those who seek earthly immortality. Whether they use alchemy, magic, or will-power, their methods always come down to the process of chasing the spirit of a man out of a young and vigorous body in order to install themselves in that body. Thus, no matter how sublime their motives seem to be, they are guilty of a more cowardly murder than the one committed by the vulgar murderer. But happily, we do not have to know about these cases of conscience.

CHAPTER II

Spiritual Correspondences

HEN HE WENT up on the mountainside, and passed the whole night offering prayer to God; and when day dawned, he called to him those whom it pleased him to call, choosing out of twelve of them whom he called his apostles to go out preaching at his command, with power to cure diseases and to cast out devils.

The names of the twelve he chose were: Simon to whom he gave the name of Peter; James, the son of Zebedee, and his brother John, to whom he gave the fresh name of Boanerges, which means: sons of thunder. The others were: Andrew, brother of Simon-Peter; Philip; Bartholomew; Matthew; Thomas; James, the son of Alphaeus; Thaddeus; Simon the Canaanite, the one known as the Zealot; and Judas Iscariot, the one who betrayed him.

And now he came into a house, and once more the multitude gathered so that the had no room even to sit and eat. His relatives having heard of it came to take him. In fact, they said that he had lost his mind.

At this time, Jesus was walking through the cornfields on the sabbath day. And his disciples, who were hungry, fell to plucking the ears of corn and eating them. The Pharisees saw this, and said to him: "Look, thy disciples are doing a thing which it is not lawful to do on the sabbath." Whereupon he said to them: "Have you never read of what David did, when he and his followers were hungry? How, during the time of the high priest Abiatar, he went into the tabernacle, and

THE HEALINGS OF CHRIST

ate the loaves set out there before God, although neither he nor his followers, nor any one else except the priests, had a right to eat them. Have your not read in the law that the priests violate the sabbath rest in the temple, and none blames them? (Numbers 28:9) And I tell you there is one standing here who is greater than the temple. If you have found what the words mean, 'It is mercy, not sacrifice, that wins favor with me,' you would not have passed judgment on the guiltless!" And he added: "The sabbath has been made for man and not man for the sabbath. That is why the Son of Man is Lord of the sabbath day."

So he went on his way, and afterwards came into the synagogue. And here, there was a man who had one of his hands withered. The scribes and Pharisees asked Jesus whether it was lawful to do a work of healing on the sabbath, so that they might have a charge to bring against him. But he answered, "Is there a man among you that has but one sheep, who would not take hold of it and pull it out, if it should fall into a pit on the sabbath? And of what value is a sheep compared to a man? There is nothing unlawful, then, in doing a work of mercy on the sabbath day." Thereupon he said to the man who had his hand withered: "Rise up and come forward!" The man rose to his feet, then Jesus said to them, "I have a question to ask you: Which is right, to do good on the sabbath day, or to do harm? To save life, or to make away with it?"

As they kept silent, he looked around on them all, with indignation, at such blindness of heart; so he said to the man: "Stretch out thy hand." As he did so, his

Spiritual Correspondences

hand was restored to him. Thereupon the Pharisees left the synagogue and plotted together with the Herodians on how to do away with him.

Jesus withdrew, with his disciples, towards the sea of Tiberias; and great crowds followed him from Galilee, and from Judea, and from Jerusalem, and from Idumaea, and from beyond Jordan; and those who lived about Tyre and Sidon, hearing of all that he did, came in great numbers to him. So he told his disciples to keep a boat ready at need because of the multitude, for fear they should press on him too close; for he did many works of healing, so that all those who were visited with suffering thrust themselves upon him, to touch him, because from him exuded a virtue that healed them all. The unclean spirits, too, whenever they saw him, would fall at his feet and cry out, "Thou art the Son of God"; and he would give them strict charge not to make him known.

This he did to fulfill the word spoken by the prophet Isaiah, "Behold, my servant, whom I have chosen, my elect, with whom my soul is well pleased. I will lay my spirit upon him, and he shall proclaim judgment among the Gentiles. He will not protest and cry out; none shall hear his voice in the streets. He will not snap the staff that is already crushed, or put out the wick that still smoulders, until the time comes when he crowns his judgment with victory. And the Gentile nations will put their trust in his name."

Then they brought him to a man possessed, who was both blind and dumb; whom he cured, giving him both speech and sight. The multitudes were filled with amazement. "Can this man," they asked, "be no other than the Son of David?" But the Pharisees and scribes who had come from Jerusalem said, when they heard of it: "It is only the power of Beelzebub, by the prince of the devils, that he casts the devils out." Whereupon Jesus, who knew what was in their thoughts, said to them, "How can Satan cast out Satan? No kingdom can be at war with itself without being laid waste; no city or household that is at war with itself can stand firm. If it is Satan who casts Satan out, then Satan is at war with himself, and how is his kingdom to stand firm? He is at his very end. Again, if it is through Beelzebub that I cast out devils, by what means do your own sons cast them out? It is for these, then, to pronounce judgment on you. But if, when I cast out devils, I do it through the spirit of God, then it must be that the kingdom of God has already appeared among you. How is anyone to gain entrance into the house of the strong man and plunder his goods without first making the strong man his prisoner? Only then can he plunder his house at will! He who is not with me, is against me; he who does not gather his store with me, scatters it abroad.

"And now I tell you this; there is pardon for all the other sins and blasphemies of men, but not for blasphemy against the Holy Spirit. Anyone who blasphemes against the Son of Man may find forgiveness, either in this world or in the world to come. Believe me, there is pardon for all the other sins of mankind and the blasphemies they utter; but if a man blas-

Spiritual Correspondences

phemes against the Holy Spirit, there is no pardon for him in all eternity; he is guilty of a sin that is eternal. And I say this, that on the Day of Judgment men will be brought to account for every thoughtless word they have spoken. Thy words will be matter to acquit, or matter to condemn thee."

Then his mother and brethren came and sent a message to him, calling him to them, while they stood without. There was a multitude sitting round him when they told him, "Behold, thy mother and thy brethren are without, looking for thee." And he answered them, "Who is my mother, who are my brethren, to me?" Then, extending his hand over his disciples, he said, "Here are my mother and my brethren! If anyone does the will of my Father, who is in heaven, he is my brother, and sister, and mother.

"When the unclean spirit, which has possessed a man goes out of him, it walks about the desert looking for a resting place, and finding none says: 'I will go back to my own dwelling, from which I came out.' And it comes back, to find that dwelling empty, and swept out, and neatly set in order. Thereupon, it goes away, and brings in seven other spirits more wicked than itself to bear it company, and together they enter in and settle down there; so that the last state of that man is worse than the first. So it shall fare with this wicked generation!"

When he spoke thus, a woman in the multitude said to him aloud: "Blessed is the womb that bore thee, the breast which thou has sucked." But Jesus answered:

THE HEALINGS OF CHRIST

"Shall we not rather say: 'Blessed are those who hear the word of God and keep it.'"[1]

Our Integrity

WHEN YOU PERUSE these commentaries, you will no doubt find them rather disconnected; but it cannot be otherwise. Time is lacking to expound, in a didactic fashion, all the horizons the gospel lays bare. You must already have discovered this to be true, as my capacities are limited. That is why these discourses resemble somewhat the explanations of a guide who, from a mountain peak, merely points out to the tourists two summits on the left, a valley behind, a river to the right, a forest here, a plateau over there. The good man does not know how to speak upon the subject methodically, but the city-dwellers who are well informed are able to coordinate their explanations and quickly establish the topography of the panorama spread out before them. So please be like these excursionists; be content with the few scattered details I can give you, and make of them a whole as best you can. This being established, let us return to the study of spiritual powers.

The theorem of these notions is that it is the spirit that governs matter—the spirit being like its center of gravity. And the biological equilibrium of matter depends upon its good relationship with the spirit. This law is verified in the collective being, as explained previously, as well as in the

---

[1] Mark 3:13–19; Luke 6:12–16; Matthew 10:1–4; 12:1–21; Mark 2:23–3:25; Luke 6:1; Matthew 12:22–32; Mark 3:22–32; Luke 11:14–15, 17–23; 12:10; Matthew 12:32, 37; Mark 3:31–35; Luke 8:19–21; Matthew 12:46–50; Luke 11:24–28; Matthew 12:43–45.

Spiritual Correspondences

individual being. One can apply the parable of the house invaded during the absence of its owner to this particular case. Among other things, the house signified the body and the physical faculties in which our spirit dwells. It is wise to remain in our house, for if we leave it, a thief may enter. The thieves may be mental diseases. Or else one can bring back from these journeys some morbid germs, these being physical diseases. Because, please do remember that any intellectual search is a sortie of the spirit: it may be a more or less conscious one, and it may be of short or long duration.

The Vocation of the Twelve

WHETHER YOU GO inside yourself to draw up a plan for a new industrial enterprise, to gather the elements for a work of art, to find collaborators, to establish your own line of conduct, or to construct your system in the world—for all of these preparations or recapitulations, unless you retire to a mountaintop first and spend your nights in prayers to God, you will not achieve anything worthwhile.

There are other mountains besides those found in geography books, other nights besides those of astronomy, other solitudes besides physical isolation—and all are as real as our Alps, our physical shadows, and our hermitages. On the other hand, there are no manifestations of our conscious being that, in order to reach perfection, do not require preparation. And, as any act is but a remote copy of one of the gestures of the Word-made-man (the One known as the *pure act* personified), any preparation can but rather poorly imitate the mysterious retreats of the Word himself, the Word-clothed-human-nature. But to prepare oneself for any contingency proves to be a very difficult task when one wants to do it thoroughly: everything is so complex, so diffused. There is so much apprehension and incertitude, unless one is either of limited intelligence or is possessed by the fire of genius. So, let us analyze this a bit further.

First of all, let us try to resemble our perfect model, Christ, in whom contemplative sublimity and realizing vigor are combined. To achieve this, our whole existence must be one of continuous preparation (through repentance, humility, good works, a desire for the ultimate) by means of a discipline to which we subject our intentions and words, as well by means of the innocence of our sentiments. Further, we must examine the reasonable purpose of our enterprise. If, then, the enterprise still seems worthy, we will ask heaven to use us to set this plan in motion only if *it* so pleases. Finally, we will establish this plan in all of its details, using all the means within our knowledge and experience.

Once this work is terminated (in the solitude of inner summits) we will turn towards the inaccessible perfection that we do not know, and will convince ourselves that, before it, our efforts are as nothing.

This very simple awareness of facts must not unduly disturb our confidence. From out of this nothingness, then, our prayer will ascend, direct, ingenuous, certain of being answered. And grace will descend in the form of intuition or strength, conformable to the nature of our products. Then, leaving our mountain, we will re-enter ordinary life, choosing our clans, our methods, our plans, our thoughts, just as Jesus did when he designated his apostles. However, this example is no more than similar to its original. It does not quite conform to its model. It does not claim to show anything but a very small way of utilizing the lessons that the acts of Jesus teach us. This is my conception, at any

Spiritual Correspondences

rate. Better for you to analyze and examine this matter as it presents itself to you.

From time's origin, the incarnation of the Word had been foreseen in all of its details, its journeying, its consequences. At the very beginning, the souls of the apostles had been chosen, together with their cosmic itineraries and individual tasks. Why then, when Jesus decides to take them with him, does he feel the need to climb the mountain to meditate over his choice, in order (or so it seems) to ask for an inspiration that, after all, is his constantly, that is certain at all times and in all planes?

Let us realize that when looking at others we see nothing but distorted appearances or images. We imagine that the motives impelling our neighbors to act as they do are the very ones that would impel us to act in the same way. But this is not always correct, especially when the being we observe is a superior being, one far more advanced than we. So, if the acts of Christ engender thousands and thousands of results, among which our limited vision enables us to discern but three or four, it is reasonable to surmise that the motive powers of Christ are far more numerous than our analyses can ever discover.

Moreover, divine prescience does not imply the slavery of any being. Our philosophers seem always to believe that God only possesses limited resources, just as they do. A grain of sand, for instance, suffices to cause our most ingenious machines to stop; and when faced with unexpected happenings, even the most fertile of brains may only work out a few expedient measures. But the Father possesses on all occasions an infinite number of solutions for an infinite number of problems; if he chooses a world, or a people, or a man to fulfill some task, and then at a certain moment this creature rebels, can he not suddenly take another, anyone at all, to fulfill that work, and endow that creature with the necessary faculties? Because his foresight, prevision, and providence are perfect, no accident due to the relative state can ever find them at fault. Ah! never will we be modest enough, let us not forget that! Our most magnificent gifts are still nothing but gifts, just as our finest virtues are. And so, perhaps this long nocturnal meditation of Jesus looking his apostles over was a revision of providential designs, a reparation for unknown defaults, a provision for new eventualities, and many other things—a thousand other things.

The Twelve were of course very old spirits, rich in experiences, ripened through long, assiduous works, "broken in" by numerous trials and tribulations. Something within them came from the old prophets of the Ancient Law who had announced the coming of the Messiah. But their whole past, so full and rich in view of their Christic mission, was worth only as much as the rough clay from which the sculptor's genius molds a sublime statue. No matter how great they had become in comparison with other human spirits, no matter how venerable or wise (such that eternal Wisdom could make use of them), there had to be a complete turnabout of their small human grandeur and inadequate human wisdom. So it seems that the night Jesus spent at the Mountain of Tiberias was used for this recasting. This, by the way, is one of the reasons why the Father takes away from his ambassadors the notion of their spiritual identity, and the memory of their past lives.

In this disconcerting night, maintaining a cheerful faith is the first gift to arm the apostles. The apostles have had to forget much, but they have learned that light comes and goes almost always in an illogical manner, bursting forth

Spiritual Correspondences

suddenly with no apparent connection with our efforts, our laziness, or our tribulations. The servant of Christ well knows this, and smiles as serenely to radiant day as he does to frightful darkness. Though still capable of succumbing, his serenity already constitutes a rare privilege. Do not, however, mistake this serenity with Buddhist impassivity or Stoic aloofness, any more than Christian unknowing resembles philosophical Scepticism.

If, when analyzing our certitudes and our doubts back to the axioms from which these are derived, we imagine the opposite axioms, we will be able to deduce a divergent line of reasoning just as logical as the first. Such dialectical exercise, which the Hindus practiced before the Greeks and Latins, brings us to the conclusion that everything is plausible and possible, but uncertain. The eclectics and dilettantes are mistaken, however: their hesitancy between thesis and antithesis in fact signifies that they have not been able to find the third, conciliatory, point of view—synthesis.

The Christian philosopher utilizes this research by establishing himself in the mystical poverty of the intellect. Through analogous exercises, the servant of God arrives at the mystical poverty of the heart. And as soon as one or the other can sincerely say "I am nothing" or "I can do nothing," the light descends, varying in purity in direct ratio to the depth of his unknowing or the emptiness of his self-will. This is the fundamental character of the soldier of Christ. To spread the good tidings (to "apostolate") is but one of his functions. He has still to effect great sacrifices and bear heavy loads before being able to receive a rank in the army of light. And he will have to perform yet further works before becoming a free-man. But we need not classify the members of the mystical phalanx. It suffices us to know its

THE HEALINGS OF CHRIST

hierarchy in general—and this for the sole reason of not taking ourselves for what we are not.

There is direct opposition between the grandeurs on earth and the powers of heaven. The heralds of God always go to the humble, the poor, the maimed, the tainted ones: those referred to as the common herd, as being "outside the pale." But this is not in order to collect more adherents to the "cause" (as sociologists would call it); it is because the common man is more worthy of help than are the ruling classes; and because, having his heart freer from ambition or avarice, the common man is more accessible to accepting truth. It is also because he has less arrogance, because he helps his neighbor more easily, because he has less leisure time than the rich to educate himself; because life is difficult for him; and, finally, because the whole world has more or less exploited him.

The apostles came from the little people. They were middling men from poor surroundings. The one with the best position among them was Matthew, the tax assessor, and yet that occupation was universally frowned upon. But, these people of little apparent account were old souls. They had gone through numerous incarnations. They had perceived the glory of the Lord and had accompanied him during his long descent throughout the numberless planetary orbs. Their immediate and simple obedience to the first call of the Master proves that they had already been chosen. Find the employee today who would give up his job, his salary, and his pension in order to follow another man as badly regarded and as misunderstood by "right-thinking" people as was Jesus at that time! So, let us never judge anyone.

But all this is still nothing. It may be that shortly (an hour from now, on the street, or perhaps a century hence

Spiritual Correspondences

some place, sometime), Jesus or one of his friends will pass by you and say: "Follow me." Believe me, at that moment, all the realities of earth will vanish. You will follow him without hesitation, because the light within us recognizes the light without. But if we want this to happen, we must be mindful of our limitations and not believe ourselves healthier than we are. We must try to cure our ills. And the doctor will come, so that neither the lame nor the sinner be offered in holocaust to justice—for his medicine is mercy. Those who believe themselves to be saintly, or just not in need of the Master, will one day recognize their error.

Before proceeding, let us pause to recall that a twelve-foldness of close disciples is to be found within all ancient initiations: in Lamaism, Brahmanism, Mazdeism, Judaism, and Orphism, as well as in the equivalent initiations of Peru, China, Thrace, and Norway.

Among the twelve around Jesus, John was the youngest. Tradition calls him "the beloved," and "the virgin." According to the gnostics, John represents charity (love), as his brother James represents hope, and Peter faith.[2] Bartholomew, the twin brother of Thomas, is one and the same as Nathan: his name means "God-given." Thaddeus or Lebbaeus means "the loving one." James (the Less) and Simon the Zealot were the "brothers" of Christ. As to the Ischariot, his name may come from Sakar ("salary"), from Iscara ("strangulation"), or from Iscoreti ("leather belt").

---

[2] Pseudo-Cyprian (*De Singularitate Clericorum*), Pseudo-Athanasius (*Dialogi* III *de Sancta Trinitate*), Saint Basil (*De Contubernalibus*) apply to all the apostles the term Boanerges ("sons of thunder") that the gospels give to John and James (Mark 3:17). Only the latter deserve this name, on account of their kinship with Jesus.

THE HEALINGS OF CHRIST

These twelve also represent, in the world, an equal number of rays from the Word; and in man, an equal number of faculties that influence the mystical life of the regenerated one.

These apostles were, or rather are (since their spirit is still alive around their Master), highly evolved beings. But they had never entered heaven. They were, in the depths of time, men who evolved through hardships and sorrow (just as we all do) so as to pay their debts to nature; men who spoke to others of God and received death as recompense. And yet, when they returned two thousand years ago they knew not who they were. What a lesson for our so-called science!

Furthermore, the evangelists offer the true principles of a community. "Any kingdom, divided against itself, will perish." Hence, spiritual unity is indispensable to the life of a communal movement. Whenever men amass currencies, or accumulate erudition, or gather in large numbers, all they are really doing is granting to time the occasion of exercising its dissolving power.

I will go as far as to say that for a group to live it is not even necessary that its members know one another, or that there be a visible head. It suffices that a collectivity unflinchingly actualizes the spiritual principle that is the soul of its foundation. The eminent example of such an association is the one the Rosicrucians have called the Church of the Holy Spirit—the same which other mystics, and even certain Fathers of the Church, have named the Interior Church (which we have mentioned previously).

So, do not spend your energies trying to round up a great many acquaintances, to discuss statutes, to establish regulations, or to send out circulars. The highest ideal you can evoke is Christ. Do his will, each for all. You may rest

Spiritual Correspondences

assured that those impelled with the same enthusiasm as yours will someday be called to join you, and that you will all be united through the harmonious effect of your love for Christ.

The Conduct of Missionaries

THIS IS ONE of the important points I feel must be called to the attention of all mystics. In many places in the gospel we read that Christ authorizes his apostles to provide for their sustenance on a sabbath day, or to receive it from those to whom they bring the light. Let us not forget that here we refer to those made apostles (which means exceptional beings entrusted with serving the light) not through their own will but through the will of heaven. Let us not believe ourselves equal to them. To become enthusiastic about the poetical conception of a servant of God wandering the world, following what he imagines to be his inspiration, and expecting (as if it were his due!) that all the people he meets will come to his aid and fill his needs, would almost be a misuse of trust. Even St Paul, though giving to those who teach the gospel (in accord with the words of our Savior) the right of living from the gospel, compelled *himself* to follow a manual trade so that, as he clearly expressed it, he would not be dependent upon anyone. But St Pauls are rare. Whenever we have done a little kindness for someone, we believe we have acted as servants of Christ. Well, one should see what the inner life of the soldiers of heaven *really* is in order to understand the intensity of their efforts: recall that even close relatives hardly appreciate their efforts, because "no man is a prophet in his own country." But if we remember that on the one hand it is written that "At thy time of fasting, anoint thy head and wash thy face so that thy fast may not be known to men" (Matthew 6:17–18), and that on the other hand the ministry of prayer requires constant spiritual fasting, we can imagine that no temporal ruler, no statesman, is charged with more concern than such an obscure Christian living apparently in middle-class fashion, but to whom, in secret, God has entrusted some work for the advancement of his brethren. No matter how vast our hopes, how ardent our desire for good may be, the humble and wise rule of conduct that must be one's code of life will make us remain just where providence has placed us, cheerfully accepting the most monotonous tasks, because they too have need of receiving light through our example. If heaven wants us somewhere else, heaven will easily direct circumstances to let us know God's will in as simple and definite a manner as our supervisor does when giving us an order at the factory.

So, pray for the sick, give a helping hand to the needy, console the afflicted, pray for public needs, give your viewpoint as a Christian whenever someone asks for it—but keep your profession and earn your family's daily bread with your labor until such time as God will decide otherwise.

God's child is beyond any law, because he became a child of God only after he had obeyed all laws, and because his heart lives in the world whence all laws come. He serves his Lord; and service to the Lord follows but one simple law: charity. Consequently, any rule or custom is obliterated before the demands of charity. On the other hand, the common man needs to exercise prudence; he must not subject his body to excessive strains, nor deprive his family of their needs, unless they are totally willing, because nothing is really his. He is but a manager, the steward, of his house,

Spiritual Correspondences

of his children, of his employees, of his domestic animals—and he will bear the responsibility of any excessive work he might impose upon anyone: "imprudence is permitted only to the soldier of Christ."

Even Jesus conforms himself to this rule of opportunity and prudence. Most of the time, when some being recognizes him, he orders him to keep quiet. In fact, nothing is more serious to a being than these recognitions of the spiritual identity concealed beneath a physical form. One can make a mistake; one may take a mental or fluidic emanation for pure light, according to whether one lives in the mental or fluidic realm. One must be humble to see the light.

Today, there are many human sages who have already poisoned Europe and America with so-called Christian theories. They are but forerunners of the still more fascinating and multitudinous sages of Asia, which this enticing Asia holds in reserve in her temples, in her deserts, and upon her sacred mountain peaks. Yes, most of these know who Christ is, but although they think themselves free, they are slaves to their systems, and so pride prevents them from acknowledging him publicly. The demons of yore who, through the mouth of the possessed ones, would scream out before Jesus: "Thou art the Son of God!"—called out because their testimony was wrought by the splendor of his virtue, which was unbearable to their benighted minds. But these adepts of Asia are men; they are freer than demons. But their freedom is different: they possess the redoubtable privilege of being able to reason, to make inferences, and, if they so choose, to shutter their minds to evidence.

Let not their blindness scandalize us. Many of us act in the same manner as these "superhumans": we often enough mistake prestige for miracle, and see something marvelous where only the divine operates. Many of Jesus's contemporaries saw him only as a magician, an agitator, a kabbalist, or a healer. Let us beware of being among those who, having met a physical personation of Our Lord on earth, will not recognize it at all on the Day of Judgment, when it will be asked of us to render account of the treasures that were entrusted to us.

On the other hand, the kindness of the Father is such that he veils any torch of light whose brilliance might risk injuring our tender eyes. When Jesus does not want to publicize his title of Son of God, it is merely because of his solicitude on our behalf: he wants to be, for the crowd, nothing but the servant of the Father, without giving rise to any suspicion of his rank among these servants. He wants to appear to be just one of the elect—a man God has chosen among others—whom the Father loves, and whom he loads with his gifts. But Jesus does not want it seen that he is the first among the servants of God, that he is their principle and their strength, that he is the elect *par excellence*, the beloved above all others, that he is capable of receiving all of the gifts of the Father, *ad infinitum*, because he himself is of the same nature as the Infinite; that, alone among all servants, he can receive the plenitude of the Spirit because he is the equal of the Spirit; and that, if all the servants are someday to judge one corner or the other of the world (which means to recognize it), he alone—Jesus—will judge the whole universe and the aggregate of all nations.

The text of Isaiah, to which the evangelist refers the reader, conclusively proves such special regard and tolerant indulgence towards us. In fact, the elect of the Lord is the beloved because he is the only one who accomplishes God's will perfectly; that is why he possesses the plenitude of celestial life. Knowing full well that discussions only serve to feed self-pride, he never argues—for he knows that truth becomes firmly embedded in us only after our efforts towards goodness, not in the wake of intellectual research. The elect of God does not clamor in city squares, he does not seek popularity. Light enters into the heart of man in silence and from within. With solicitude, the elect of the Lord nurse the semi-broken boughs of our enfeebled faculties and patiently revive the faint glimmer (ever nearing extinction) of our agonizing hearts. Because man perfects himself only through his bold efforts, he understands only what he has experienced. He appreciates the worth of a thing only after having tasted its dregs. Advice and admonishment are worthless to him—he never believes in them, except in part. That is why Jesus Christ, the elect of God, prior to addressing his moving discourses to us on earth (and before giving us the *precept*), took care to give us first the *example* by means of the frightful sacrifice of his descent down-here, and his martyrdom.

So, let us exert ourselves to do good and act accordingly, rather thank give discourses: our example will be far more convincing; our action that much more kind and healthy; and the fruits of our apostolate more numerous.

Divine Things and Public Opinion

PROVERBS as well as superstitions occasionally raise some particular remarks erroneously to the undue level of general truths. Thus, it rarely happens that the voice of the people is the voice of God. To render this adage veridical, one would have to establish a difference between the people and the crowd. One might say that the word "crowd" represents

THE HEALINGS OF CHRIST

all the classes of society linked and bound, under the influence of some kind of inebriation, by their lower instincts; while to the word "people" we attribute a healthier, more alive, and a profounder meaning, almost synonymous with what we recently referred to as the laboring classes. Hence, the people would be the ensemble of those through whom the nation lives: basically, the manual laborers are its foundation, but equally so are its administrative and intellectual workers. Both the common laborer and the farmer are inclined to refer to the white-collar workers as lazy; and yet there are many middlemen, engineers, managers, scientists, doctors, and artists who daily put in sixteen hours of work rather than only eight, and who become just as exhausted as the miners and rail-splitters do. Muscular fatigue is indubitably painful, but nervous fatigue wears one out just as much. Moreover, any task pursued to its very limits confers mystical nobility and draws to us the light from the Real.

Also, because they live with energy and propagate life, the people recognize the torchbearers, whereas the crowd vilifies them on account of their interfering with its impulsive whims: its jeering rises all the more furious in proportion as popular acclamations rise the more enthusiastic in step with the purity and generosity with which the light shines.

Alone among all those heralds, Jesus always arouses extreme oppositions: thought of as son of God by some, as son of Beelzebub by others; believed to be of unsound mind by his relatives, he overthrows everything before reorganizing everything.

The people, all who concern themselves with familial responsibility and shoulder social duty, i.e., the working-nation, discern the light because they carry within themselves healthy faculties: first, energy, which means having

Spiritual Correspondences

the courage not to spare any effort; then common sense, the sense of what is real and alive. This is just, because in order to receive new forces one must first spend the ones one possesses, because the integrity one lives by proffers a right appraisal of things and people. Jesus sides with the people, for regardless how subtle the Pharisaic arguments may be, he never opposes to them anything but good common sense. When he is accused of chasing demons away with the help of the prince of demons, his reply is: "Would Satan become his own enemy? You accept the fact that hell seeks to escape? Then it must be that heaven has descended upon you."

We are led in this manner towards the great simplification that extricates our reason-encumbered intellect and augments our power to act. God or the devil, good or evil, charity or selfishness: these necessary pairings suffice to direct us—no more hesitations, no more compromises, no more sparing of self. There are two camps only, and between them the space is empty. If we do not side with Christ, we are immediately drafted by the devil, who will even grab any who do not give themselves completely and explicitly to Christ. Whoever works for any other goal than to serve Christ, no matter how beautiful and plentiful are the fruits of their labor… they rot.

Here is one of the practical reasons for which faith in Christ as being both God and Man seems to me so terribly important. In the tumult of the innumerable movements that constitute universal existence, quality outweighs quantity. Moreover, things can only receive two qualities: they are either divine or natural. And as it is the intention behind the act that "qualifies" it, any act that does not have Christ as its objective must die after a time (whether it be short or long) because the Word alone confers supernaturalness. When looking into the future at this same conglomeration of acts, one can see most of them dissipating their fruits at the caprice of extraneous circumstances, whereas on the other hand some acts (too few, however) group their results together; they coordinate and organize them, thus perpetuating themselves far into the future, because they have been launched in the name of Christ and for his service alone.

All those who follow this discipline of intentions admit that it is just as difficult as it is important. Energy, perseverance, and vigilance do not suffice, for rarely are we in accord with ourselves, given that several wills, some good, some bad, wrestle within us, each ruling in turn, or occasionally a few ruling together, so that we become agitated by contradicting ourselves. Have you not noticed how our acts differ from our words, for instance? One man may swear and blaspheme, but his anger happily does not reach his fist, while another holds such a lofty discourse, yet commits a thousand misdeeds! We are neither totally good nor totally bad—we zigzag—but God esteems neither cowardice nor cleverness; we have to become homogeneous.

Jesus knows well our human flaw, the cause of both our present misery and our future greatness. He wishes to help us rebuild our unity, by establishing within us that unitary heaven evocative of the eternal Kingdom where all are one, in themselves and with each other. He misses no opportunity to teach us to simplify ourselves, to reduce all the gestures of our inner life under the obedience of the same principle, by a single method, towards the same goal. Thus, after having established the great universal antinomies that we have just mentioned, and after having demonstrated that the realization of our own unity will occur by uniting our-

Spiritual Correspondences

selves to him—the absolute corporated Unity—he leads us to the conquest of our psychological unification by means of two lessons that apparently seem foreign to this objective: the one lesson being the importance of the spoken word; the other, our spiritual parentage. There must be harmony with ourselves within ourselves, then harmony between ourselves and our fellow-beings—a twin goal towards which our Master leads us indirectly. He knows us to be indocile and vain; his tenderness wants to spare us revolt and discouragement, and to earn the small merits of a slightly longer search: the long road is easier than the shortcut.

Before placing himself face to face with one of the forms of the absolute, man must forget everything belonging to the relative state, he must make of his brain a clean sheet, and of his heart, that of a child. So, before undertaking the two lessons aforesaid, Jesus chases despair away from us when he announces the forgiveness of all sins, of all blasphemies, except the sin against the Holy Ghost. This exception should not frighten us, because such a sin is impossible for us to commit: the Spirit remains inaccessible to any nonregenerated creature. Of the three divine Persons, Christ is closest to us, and yet no one knows him, no one even will know him before that day when the doors of heaven will open. The Father remains still more unfathomable, and the Spirit even more so (if I may use such meager words to express myself). He who would attack the Spirit could attack him only because he would have seen everything, learned everything, and experienced everything. Hence, his attack would be like some sort of suicide of his entire being, because he would be launching himself into nothingness. The truth is that what our sublimest contemplatives have said of the Spirit is nil. Let us be concerned only about the faults we do understand, as it is these for which we are held fully responsible.

To go with God or to choose the devil, that we do understand—we are responsible for that choice. When we attack Christ, we know what we are doing—we are responsible for that act. Our words may express our true sentiments, or lie; we can speak evil about others; we can speak with no aim in view—we are fully conscious of all this, and know we are fully responsible for all this, and that on Judgment Day we will have to render account for our slightest word. This warning of condemnation does not contradict the promise of forgiveness stated here above. In order to forgive, in fact, one has to have been subjected to the offense—and the Father does not take offence at our revolts. For a while, he lets us experience the misfortunes resulting from such revolts; but then, as soon as he notices that we are truly repentant and have the will to do better, he forgives us, which means he cleanses our heart and corrects all the disorders our sin had engendered in us—in our body, in our surroundings, in the visible as well as in the invisible world. To receive the forgiveness of heaven is a grave and marvelous favor. Let us be careful not to lose it. Let us watch over our thoughts, over our words, over our acts. To control our gestures is relatively easy; to control our thoughts, which spontaneously gush from our heart, is almost impossible. If we want to give ourselves a little trouble, let us try to control our words; little by little, through this secret discipline, we will get the crowd around us to insult less what they do not understand.

Spiritual Correspondences

The Spoken Word

WE ARE NOT aware of what a year, a month, or one single day represent; but when we will have repaired to the land of the dead, the terrestrial time we often waste will seem to us of inestimable value. As you see, I always come back to voluntary effort; do not fear that by following a strict discipline you will dry the sources of inspiration and enthusiasm within you.

The faintest breath from the Spirit wafting over us surpasses by far the most gigantic efforts we can exert to conquer the self. So, without any inconvenience, we can harness all our physical, moral, and intellectual faculties to become subservient to the gospel.

Among all these powers, there is one that most people on earth abuse, and that belongs to terrestrial man: the spoken word. Almost everywhere, creatures have some other means of expressing themselves; but here on earth, speech occupies a central post in the mechanism of life. That is why the law promulgates this decree: "By thy words shall thou be justified, and by thy words thou shalt be condemned." (Matthew 12:37) In our present state, in fact, we are held less responsible for our acts than we are for our words, and still less for our thoughts, over which we have hardly any control.

Our thoughts spring from the heart, in spite of us. All we can do, when they are bad, is not dwell on them—the time necessary to put our acts into realization may be used for reflection. It also happens that we do wrong while meaning to do right. Moreover, an act, good or bad, demands the collaboration of a great number of prescient energies about which we are not conscious: we do not know, we are ignorant of, what our ancestors have deeded to us; we are not at all masters of our physical life; we are ignorant about most of our secret life.

On the other hand, we do know what we *say*; we can govern our tongue far better than we can control the thousands of obscure movements of the rest of our body. And these words, so quickly formed, spring directly out of our heart. They are alive and immortal—alas! for most of them are idle or unkind words.

Let us be aware that in the beginning speech was given to man in order to create in the image of the Father. I dare not tell all the marvels our words could have produced, had we not misused them. Now we must reascend the incline. It will be difficult, but will we not try?

So, no more unkind words, no unnecessary remarks. We should reach the stage of not abusing any creature: not weather, mud, or a bothersome animal; not the tool we have awkwardly handled; much less, not our fellowmen. As to theories, let us confine our remarks to whether they seem to conform or not to our understanding of what we hold to be the truth. As for criminals or wrongdoers, let us find excuses for them. Yes, Christ stigmatized the Pharisees, the vendors, and the hypocrites, but we are not Christ.

At our side there stands constantly both a good angel and an evil angel, who see and hear everything we do and say. The good angels band together, the bad ones are often separated. When we speak ill of a being who cannot defend himself, either because he is absent or because he belongs to another kingdom than ours, his angel is there to see and hear us. At the minimum, three angels of the light are witnesses to our maliciousness, which separates us from them and intercepts the light. Though they would like to, these angels cannot help us. Each slander adds another brick to

Spiritual Correspondences

the wall we erect between them and us. We separate ourselves from heaven. We condemn ourselves. Then we leave our interlocutors, and that's three, four, or more couples of divided beings who could have remained united. And for harmony to be restored, we have to wait for circumstances to bring all the same people together again, and for the offended party to offer forgiveness to the one who attacked him.

As far as idle words go, they condemn us because they are a waste. Joking to cheer up a tired comrade is useful; speaking out of courtesy is right, since the disciple must consider himself inferior to anyone. But talking to make noise atrophies the power of attention, and gradually renders us incapable of following ideas.

Spiritual Families

ALL BEINGS have an analogy with or are linked to one another, no matter under what form they appear. A man has a relationship with planets; a god is connected to some form of matter or other. The science of one fraction of these correspondences constituted ancient esotericism.

The Kabbalah, for instance, delineated the philosophical anatomy of one of the gods of our present creation, Adam Kadmon. The rabbis believed that this being filled the world, though he is effectively but one of its aspects. The Brahmans on the other hand taught the embryology of the universe: a point of view comprising still more complex developments. The ancient initiates of the yellow race, who were pure intellectuals, dealt in cosmic mathematics, psychic geometry, and divine mechanics.

It is not indispensable to have familiarized ourselves with

THE HEALINGS OF CHRIST

the mental methods used by the ancient sages. If one has enough presence of mind not to become fascinated by their often misleading lustre, they constitute an excellent gymnastic that may permit some slight progress.

But we should be satisfied with the following notions. Each man belongs to an invisible family, to which the visible family into which he was born should correspond. Each group is composed of analogous individuals, which means they are endowed with the same working-tools because they have the same task, or, if you prefer, because they are on the same path. They start from the same locus of evolution and work towards the same temporary goal. The first of each group, the eldest, leads the others.

Such is the basis of all divinatory sciences; but you must recall what restrictions follow their usage.

In a given family, it is possible that one member charges ahead; and if the others cannot catch up with him, he joins a more advanced group. Also, it may be that one member sees a shortcut, where his parents cannot follow, but which permits him to gain time. There are also a great many laggards. Hence, a family is not something fixed; and certainly it is not today what it was at the beginning of the journey.

Spiritual paths are just like our roads on earth. Those connecting large cities, where life is abundant and money plentiful, skirt obstacles, are well laid out, well-paved, heavily-traveled highways. But as soon as one wants to avoid winding detours, explore unknown territories, or attempt some kind of work in a remote country, the road immediately becomes more solitary, rugged, and steep.

That is exactly what happens in the Invisible. In measure as we leave the confines of the world behind us and come closer to its center, the paths become more and more difficult to travel, and one rarely meets another traveler. All roads are laid out, but some one travels only with great anguish and trouble because of thickets, torrents, quagmires, highway robbers, and wild beasts. The courage demanded of a traveler to leave the beaten path is known mystically as "the call of the Word." Each step taken and each effort exerted by that hardy man, he can make only by and through the inexpressible force of that call. One by one, he has relinquished the walking-staff, the shoes, the apparel in fashion on the broad thoroughfares. The air of the unknown countries he is now crossing changes even the quality of his blood. The expectancy of danger sharpens his senses, his scalings and descents. His swimming across rivers has increased his forces tenfold. Just as material work done with good intentions gives health and brings about for our next life a normal and vigorous body, this steady alchemy slowly transforming the traveler throughout is the growth of Christ within him. Thus does it come to pass that the one who conforms to the will of heaven is the younger brother of Jesus, since he imitates him; that he is the mother of Jesus, because each pain, each effort, each cell that dies at the workbench, each sacrifice, transmutes a little of his opaque materiality by increasing the central light which is the Word.

Who is My Mother? Who are My Brothers?

ONE CAN VISUALIZE the world as a forest where all sorts of plants, shrubs, and trees grow, to all appearances in an inextricable state of confusion. And yet, though hidden, there is order regulating this chaos: the nature of the terrain, its incline, the rate of flow of the waters, of the winds, and of the light either favor or prevent the germination of the seeds and their growth. The same applies to the forest of the human race, with the particularity that we are double plants, both terrestrial and celestial, sinking our roots into the physical below, into the humus of destiny; and from above, by contrast, descending from the spiritual—but producing both kinds of flowers in the light of day. Thus, whatever work we devote ourselves to, whether manual trade or metaphysical calling, art or science, realization or speculation—its fruits partake of heaven and earth. Also, as to ourselves, built out of elements anterior to evolution, atavism, and heredity, we see ourselves completed by a double descent into the present. Higher cosmic forces come to the cradle of each child, and, in addition, a supernatural light, a divine grace, is offered him through the ministry of his angel.

There are three factors for every creature: the evolutional forces of the past, the present force of the individual, the involutional forces of the supraterrestrial worlds. But where man is concerned there is a fourth factor: the divine gift that Christ offers us, but that we do not always accept.

So, next to each cradle, two long processions of parents are conjoined: the lineage as to the flesh; the lineage as to the spirit. If the world mechanism had not been warped by the innumerable disobediences of our race, these two lines of descent would coincide. Such a harmony, however, is rare, which is why we encounter such incompatibility of characters, hatreds, and variant sets of values among members of one family.

This is the general case; but there are exceptions. A nation may need a stimulant, a helper; it may have deserved an initiator or a jailer. Then, in a family whose members present

Spiritual Correspondences

the properties and faculties suitable to the task he will have to fulfill, arrives either a human spirit very, very much in advance who retraces his steps to encourage latecomers, or else some extra-human creature, a genius perhaps, a god, or perhaps a demon, who brings a new science, a great social advance, an unknown form of art; or who, on the contrary, inculcates in the crowd whom he takes hold of the hard lessons of suffering.

Let me digress here for a moment, for a very important reason. First of all, I ask you never to apply to yourself or to your children any of the vain glorifications of the exceptions mentioned above. Let me repeat once more: the spirit that on the higher spheres governs some of their functions, or that on the lower spheres excites some of their anger, that old soul, when it takes a body on earth, forgets its anterior past, little by little. This is a rigid law; no one, from the age of reason on, can lift the veil separating him from his past existences and worlds. No vision, no esoteric art, can ever let us see what we have been. In order to preserve us from the temptations of pride, or the cowardice that might prove too heavy for our weakness, or to enable supernatural faith to grow in us, or to save us from despair—for all these reasons, heaven does not want us to know our past or our future with certitude. So, let us not attempt to fathom who we are, or what this hero or genius may have been. We must not judge.

Secondly, accept, if you want to, the theory of multiple lives, or reject it: it matters not, since a Christian must not concern himself with his future, but only with the present day, and consecrate himself to perfecting all his forces. The simplest approach is not to concern yourself with reincarnation, not to preach that doctrine, nor to scrutinize its mysteries. In fact, this theory offers no precision. How could it be otherwise? We do not really know what constitutes a being, or where our energies come from. We do not know the invisible. We have forgotten our ancestors and don't know our descendants. We do not see our guides. Moreover, our paths are not individualistic, they are collective. We walk and live in groups, in spiritual families. Our elders lead us on, and we in turn must lead our younger brothers. The head of the group, the eldest of the family, can change the functions of each of its members, alter their places, and adjust their burden.

For instance, when a man dies, the ensemble of his personality contains several series of elements that one could divide into two large classes: the temporary elements that death returns to the milieu of their origin (such as the body, automatic notions, superficial energies) and the permanent elements (the profound acquisitions that augment the immortal self because they are of supraterrestrial nature). Also, it is written: "To him that has not, that much more will be taken away." Hence, if the guiding angel of this spiritual family sees that a certain attainment renders its possessor vain or avaricious, he can take it way from him, in part or totally, and give it to another member of this family. That is why the identity who reincarnates is almost never identical to himself: between his death and his rebirth he may have lost certain qualities or gathered quite a few others. There will never be two selves in one body; but what surrounds all these selves can be subjected to the most varied distribution. These apparent anomalies have the moral result of developing within us the indispensable sentiment of fraternity, since we each hold within ourselves a little of the physical or etheric particles that, in greater quantities,

Spiritual Correspondences

constitute most of our fellow beings. Spontaneous sympathies and antipathies have no other cause.

In addition (recalling that what we have thus far said pertains to the natural order), according to the supernatural order, the fruit of an existence, the light of all good deeds performed in humility, is found in, or rather is permanently attached to, the self. But if, one day, this self gives in to pride and comes to believe that this light belongs to it, heaven takes it away almost entirely and gives it to another, more humble one. Here, too, "to him who has not, it will be taken away."

These are the general laws according to which the "revolutions of souls" operate. But before us now is the singular case *par excellence* that Christ brings to this fundamental plan, wherein he confers upon his perfect disciples a possible renewal through an exceptional privilege intrinsic to the Holy Spirit.

In the midst of a social gathering, told that his mother and his brothers are asking for him, Jesus replies: "Who is my mother, and who are my brothers?" A very harsh statement from the human standpoint; but, I must admit, it is one that conforms with the reality of the facts.

Neither you nor I want to become involved in controversies; we are not seeking whether these "brothers" were actual brothers, or cousins. Catholics affirm that the holy mother of Christ never had any other children and that her virginity remained perpetual; Protestants maintain that she had several children by her husband. Who will decide between the merits of virginity and those of maternity? St Paul's advice, which one always brandishes in favor of the former, seems to me, if I dare say so, to be a defeat, because no one is certain, had he triumphed over ten thousand temptations, of not succumbing to the ten thousandth-and-one. Also, if all women refused maternity, how could the spirits who at the gates of the earth are impatiently waiting to come back and be purified through sorrow, effect their evolution? On the other hand, it is true that physical chastity does economize certain forces, which permits their being transposed into psychic works: in truth, all pre-Christian wisdom is in accord with subsequent Catholic wisdom. But these transmutations of psychic dynamics into fluidic dynamics do not reach any higher than magnetism or the mental level. They do not join the supernatural. They are hyperphysical, not divine. And then, what hairsplitter will judge whether the pains of motherhood, the vigils and anguish of a mother, so often out of proportion with the joys of conjugal love, are worth more or less than the renunciations of monastic virginity, with its struggles and rigorous penances?

But let us return to our subject.

If Jesus is God, if his terrestrial body was formed in the womb of his mother through a special operation of the Holy Spirit (and this we must believe in spite of any physiological reasoning), then he did not have anything in common with his terrestrial parents.

So why do we come to this world on the common path? To renew it, to sanctify it, to divinize it. It would be unseemly to expose these mysteries. We will know them only when we can be nothing but irreproachable friends to one another. Meanwhile, Christian couples may know that the marriage state holds within it miraculous possibilities. Christ does not hesitate to make allusions to it when he proclaims that those who put the word of God into practice are "his mother and his brothers." Heard in its plenitude, this sentence explains the secret of true regeneration.

Spiritual Correspondences

Imagine, if you can, a perfect disciple, man or woman, one who will never consider anything other than to serve God; who out of love of God will never permit himself a thought, a word, or an action that is not for the benefit of someone else; who, not merely content to undertake all the work that comes his way, will always choose, between two labors, that most challenging to his selfishness; who, lastly, when no work seems to call him, will be ingenious enough to invent one that may be for the general good. Thus, while living an existence of perpetual sacrifices, he will yet consider himself a worthless servant. In such a being, everything is transformed little by little, is regenerated and re-created. His mental faculties, his soul powers, his physical strength, down to the last globule of his blood, even to his bone-marrow, everything is cleansed, from his ancestral blots to his personal sins. To all of this, the Spirit gives new life, divine life. The Word is born in the center of that being. He becomes the father and the mother, the brother and the sister of Christ, since from then on he draws all his virtues from Christ, just as a new shoot takes its substance and its qualities from the old vine-stock upon which it has been grafted.

I hope that you will not see in these short explanations the materialism that some metaphysicians would doubtless find in them. The gospel is neither a kind of physics nor metaphysics—everyone can understand that. I dare also state that it is no more a kind of spiritualism than it is a materialism. All such viewpoints belong to human analysis, whereas the gospel is a divine glance into things, a realism—it is a unity, it contains all known systems and many others besides. Remember that God is not only all this and all that, not merely all of something combined with all of something

THE HEALINGS OF CHRIST

else, but an infinity of inconceivable modes. And remember that the gospel is the word of God.

When Christ makes a statement, everything is to be found therein: thought, feeling, act; principle, law, fact; thesis, antithesis, synthesis. Let us assimilate his teaching as a threefold sustenance: communion with the Word through intellect, through love, and by act. And the happy stasis will come when these three great ternaries themselves disappear—when to understand, to love, and to act will have become for us one simple gesture.

CHAPTER III

Reception of Grace

 S JESUS ENTERED Capernaum, a centurion came to him, asking for his aid. This centurion had a servant, very dear to him, who was at the point of death. The centurion, having heard of Jesus, sent to him elders of the Jews, who beseeched him to come and heal his servant. And when they came to Jesus, they entreated him earnestly, saying: "He is worthy and deserves that you do this for him, for he loves our nation and it is he who has built us our synagogue at his own cost." Jesus answered: "I shall go and heal him."

So Jesus went with them. And when he was already near the house, the centurion sent friends to say to him, "Lord, do not trouble thyself, for I am not worthy that thou shouldst come under my roof; that is why I did not think myself worthy to come to thee. If thou wilt only speak a word of command, my servant will be healed, for I too am a man subject to authority, and have soldiers subject to me; and when I say to one, 'Go,' he goes; and to another, 'Come,' he comes; and to my servant, 'Do this,' and he does it."

Now when Jesus heard this, he marveled, and turning to the crowd that followed him said, "Believe me when I say that not even in Israel have I found such great faith. And I tell you that many will come from the East and from the West, and will take their place and feast with Abraham, Isaac, and Jacob in the kingdom of heaven, but the children of that kingdom will be put forth into the darkness outside, where there will

THE HEALINGS OF CHRIST

be weeping and gnashing of teeth." Then Jesus said to the centurion, "Go thy way; as thou has believed, so be it done to thee." And, at that hour the servant was healed.

The following day it happened that Jesus was going to a town called Nain, attended by his disciples and by a great multitude of people. And as he drew near the gate of the town, a dead man was being carried out to his burial; the only son of his mother, who was a widow. And a large gathering from the town went with her. When the Lord saw her, he had compassion on her, and said "Do not weep!" Then he went up and put his hand on the bier. The bearers stood still, and he said, "Young man, I say to thee, arise!" And he who was dead, sat up, and began to speak. Jesus, then, gave him back to his mother.

But fear seized upon all, and they began to glorify God, saying, "A great prophet has risen among us. God has visited his people." So this report concerning him went forth throughout the whole of Judea, and all of the country roundabout.

John's disciples brought him word of all these things in his prison. So John summoned two of his disciples and sent them to the Lord, to ask: "Art thou he who is to come, or shall we look for another?"

And when the men had come to Jesus, they said, "John the Baptist has sent us to thee, saying, 'Art thou he who is to come, or shall we look for another?'" In the

Reception of Grace

very time of their visit he cured many of diseases, afflictions and evil spirits, and to many who were blind he granted sight. So he answered the messengers and said to them, "Go and report to John what you have heard and seen: the blind see, the lame walk, the lepers are cleansed, the deaf hear, the dead rise, the poor have the gospel preached to them. And blessed is he who is not scandalized in me."

Then, as the messengers of John had gone away, he took occasion to speak of John to the multitudes: "What did you go out to the desert to see? A reed trembling in the wind? A man clothed in soft garments? Behold, those who wear fine clothes and live in luxury are in the house of kings. But what did you go out to see? A prophet? Yes, I tell you, and more than a prophet. This is he of whom it is written (Malachi 3:1) 'Behold, I send my messenger before thy face, who shall make ready thy way before thee.' I tell you, that among those born of women there is not a greater prophet than John the Baptist; yet the least in the kingdom of God is greater than he. But from the days of John the Baptist until now the kingdom of heaven has opened to force, and the forceful have been seizing it by force. Whereas all the prophets and the law before John's time could only speak of things that were to come. And this I tell you, if you are willing to receive it in your mind, that he is that Elijah whose coming was prophesied.

"Listen, you that have ears to hear with! It was the common folk who listened to him, and the publicans that had given God his due, by receiving John's bap-

THE HEALINGS OF CHRIST

tism, whereas the Pharisees and the lawyers by refusing to be baptized by him, brought to naught God's purpose concerning themselves.

"To what then shall I liken the men of this generation? And what are they like? They put me in mind of those children sitting in the marketplace who call to one another and say, 'We have piped to you, and you have not danced; we have sung dirges, and you have not wept.' For when John the Baptist came, he neither ate bread nor drank wine, and you say, 'He is possessed of a devil.' When the Son of Man came, he ate and drank with you and you say: 'Behold a man who is a glutton, and a wine-drinker; he is a friend of publicans and sinners!' But wisdom is vindicated by all her children."

Then, after two days he departed from that place and returned to Galilee, for Jesus himself bore witness that a prophet receives no honor in his own country. When, therefore, he had come into Galilee, the Galileans made him welcome, because they had seen all that he had done in Jerusalem during the feast. And so he came once more to Cana of Galilee, where he had turned the water into wine.

And there was a certain royal official whose son was lying sick at Capernaum, This officer, having heard that Jesus had come from Judea into Galilee, went to him and besought him to come down and heal his son, for he was at the point of death.

Reception of Grace

Jesus therefore said to him, "Unless you see signs and wonders, you do not believe!" The royal official said to him. "Sir, come down before my child dies." Jesus answered him, "Go back home, thy son is to live." The man believed the word that Jesus spoke to him, and began his journey home. While he was still on his way down, his servants met him and brought word, saying that his son was still alive. He asked of them therefore the hour in which he had got better, and they told him, "Yesterday, at the seventh hour, the fever left him." The father knew then that it was at that very hour in which Jesus had said to him, "Thy son is to live." And he himself and his whole household found faith. Thus for the second time Jesus did a miracle upon his return from Judea to Galilee.[1]

The Centurion

IT SEEMS TO ME that the story of the centurion of Capernaum indicates all of the conditions necessary to obtain the graces of heaven. This man expresses the desire that his servant be healed, just as we wish for our faithful servants (our body and our faculties) not to suffer. He is a good man. He has helped the people with whom he came in contact, just as we must help those around us. He is humble. He does not feel worthy of coming before the Lord. He does not even feel worthy of receiving the salvational visit. He only asks for one word (knowing that distance is non-existent as far as the All-Powerful is concerned) and that no matter

---

[1] Matthew 8:5–13; Luke 7:1–10; 7:11–17; 13-30; Matthew 11:2–15; Luke 7:31–35; Matthew 11:16–19; John 4:43–54.

THE HEALINGS OF CHRIST

how far may be the place from which we call him, his presence is always immediate. These are the seven examples for us to follow.

Of course, such a faith is admirable; how happy we will be the day this faith spontaneously wells up within us! In order to obtain it, we must fulfill our duty, as the centurion did, in all simplicity. The turn of mind that shows us things in their aspect of complexity is useful, certainly, and loosens up our brains; however, it is but a school, an apprenticeship. The man whom the light touches sees plainly the complications in the world, but he does not become entangled with them. Since the living tie that binds him to unity lays bare to him in detail how it may be adjusted to the ensemble, the unforeseen does not baffle him.

So, in one glance, the centurion understood and saw Christ as a commander-in-chief who gives orders to his numerous soldiers and servants, orders they in turn execute with far better intelligence and promptitude than do those executed, however admirably, by the subalterns of the Roman officer. This man did not get lost in the forest of esoteric or religious theories; in one glance he understood that diseases are beings, that their healing is a spiritual act, that in the world of the spirit, space and time vanish, and that the word of God is life itself and pure action.

All that we can do to obtain true faith—a living, practical faith—can be summed up as: acquire the habit of holding permanent conversations with God; speak to God as if He were someone present. Let us train ourselves to achieve this. Five minutes morning and night do not suffice. Just as an adolescent constantly monitors his speech and posture, so each of the short pauses that, twenty times a day, separate our various occupations must be filled with a sudden

Reception of Grace

return to Christ; each must be used to increase our courage and to bring a central realignment into our inner self. Yes, this means a long discipline; but does not the acquisition of any mastery, even a temporal one, require similar constant restraint? Many years ago we heard it said that: "To smile in the midst of difficulties is the entrance to the path leading to faith." Such powerful serenity can unfold only through perpetual communion with God, by dint of elevating our hearts above all petty earthly vicissitudes, by soliciting a miracle and relishing our nothingness.

Humility, in fact, constitutes the nursery for faith. These sons of the kingdom, who were destined by providence to receive the living God here on earth, if they have been flung into the outer darkness, it is because of the pride they felt when finding themselves to be the "chosen people"; while as to the foreign nations that have come from the East and the West, the reason the Father admits them to his banquets is their humility.

Thus, it is by accomplishing all of our duty simply, by harboring true humility alongside constant remembrance of our Father, that faith grows; and faith, in turn, permits us to spread miracles of divine kindness all around us. So, let us go back to work. I often sense that you have an unfounded and fearful anxiety, or doubt, and that you are worried; but this sterilizes your efforts. Catch your second breath, become calm and reassured, and go back to work! What have you to fear, fatigue? You have overcome it before. Failure? But you have an excellent Master who will observe your efforts before he counts your successes. You serve the wisest of masters, and when he does not permit you to win a startling victory, it is because an apparent defeat is better for you—and for your adversaries.

THE HEALINGS OF CHRIST

The Widow's Son

GENERALLY, we lack inner plenitude, the feeling of calm joy and of serenity that arms the soul of the ascetic, just as euphoria gives buoyancy to the body of the athlete. Yet, this plenitude results from exercising in the direction, and in the field, of spiritual realities.

For instance, let us take this approximate example regarding the resurrection of the son of the widow of Nain, which extraordinary event the evangelist relates in twelve or fourteen lines. But, what profound semantic depths could each word bring forth, were we to extract from these sentences the meanings implied in each? The name of the city, the names of the disciples, the crowd, the body being carried to the burying ground, an only son of a widow, the helpers, the compassion of Jesus, and his remark: "Do not weep." Note his intervention, although no one has asked him anything of him: he comes forward, he touches the coffin, the pallbearers stop, then comes the thaumaturgic command "Rise up," Jesus "gives him back to his mother," then there is the fear in the crowd, and much else besides.

Apply each of these details to the spiritual man, to the moral man, to the intellectual man, to the ethers, to the physical man, to his daily life, to the social plane, to matter, to knowledge, to the earth, and to many other places! The widowed mother of the raised one may be likened to Creation separated from its Lord by sin, or to the Church, or to a people, or to a lost soul. One may apply many of the meanings of this episode alchemically, in mystic psychology, even in national economics. But this research, although not quite just a game of symbolism, only satisfies intellectual curiosity; to satisfy the heart, only the intuitions of the var-

Reception of Grace

ious orders of reality contained in one word, or in one of Christ's gestures, are worthwhile, for they spring spontaneously from the depths of our being when our will embraces the divine will and surrenders by molding all the conscious powers of our person to this model.

In Jesus is a unity that englobes and surpasses the universe; everything he does and everything he says shakes out the forms of space and of time. For instance, to resurrect a dead person is not a simple act: hundreds of terrestrial or supraterrestrial, visible or invisible, creatures are attached to each human being; they die with him, just as they were born with him. And so, to make a dead person live again demands that all these auxiliaries and attending companions be brought back to life as well—which means in turn that innumerable upheavals will be provoked, bringing about many more pains than joys. So-called magnetic or magic resurrections either ignore these complexities or else do not concern themselves about them. But the true mystic has to be concerned, which is why he never permits himself to perform anything beyond asking heaven's help.

For our demands to be heard, then granted, it is necessary that we live on earth and in heaven simultaneously; that we not travel back and forth, but be present up there and down here simultaneously; that we breathe both atmospheres, see both realities. That this is possible, even easy, is because, in truth, through Christ, both are one.

Let your glance, then, become more penetrating, so that the beings with whom you live will become translucid to you, so that the web of circumstances will not hide the designs of divine forces from you, so that you will find in each minute and in all places the secret spot through which each of those beings is tied to the infinite, and how each of

THE HEALINGS OF CHRIST

those forces is tied to the eternal. For the present, your regeneration has not been achieved. It has hardly begun. The light only inhabits a very small corner of your being; only in that minimal domain is plenitude yours. Hence, gradually, you have to rid yourself of the remaining unrealities that occupy it without filling it.

Look, for instance, at the crisis of the French monetary exchange of today, in which a great many of our compatriots have placed their faith. But money is only a sign, and a financial exchange a sign of a sign, which in these uncertain times finally comes to mean very little and certainly does not correspond to the true wealth of a nation. The French people have permitted themselves to be taken in by the symbol, the image, the shadow. Had they chosen to ignore the manipulations of international finance, had they acted as if these maneuvers were not in play, there would not have been in our stock exchange any of the repercussions from the undertow of Amsterdam or elsewhere: the attack against our franc would have met a void, and the attack would have been dissolved.

So it is on the spiritual level. Behave as though perishable things are all-powerful, and they will enslave you. Behave instead as though all divine things are the only real ones, and God will make you all-powerful, will fulfill your desires just as a father joyfully grants gifts and recompenses to his good child. The most intelligent and cultured religious men seldom understand or conceive these absolutes of plenitude and union; they figure that human means are also necessary to faith in order to regenerate the temporal world. That is because there are more administrators and professors than there are true mystics. I was thinking of this recently as I was reading a book by Henri Massis.

Reception of Grace

This shrewd, erudite, judicious mind with healthy Catholic leanings declares that the simple realization of each person of faith of the maxims of the gospel would not suffice, no matter how complete it might be, to renovate the social order, or to give back to a nation its prosperity, or to rectify the errors of its philosophers and artists. This can only mean that Henri Massis has never felt the all-powerfulness of the Word Jesus; that he is too intellectual to have become, or to be, simple "in the spirit"; that he still nourishes himself with unsubstantial foods; that his Christian faith is founded on the thoughts of commentators; that he studies the divine text only through glosses of the Fathers or canons of the Councils.

We are not faring any better either in the order of our daily activities. We install intermediaries between God and ourselves. We have not taken the decision of going straight to him. And even when we intend to do so, we dare not bring it to realization. This means that, when Christ comes to us, it is he who comes all the way. Just as happened to the friends and to the mother of the young man of Nain who were lamenting, not knowing that the Lord of life was passing right by them, so it is likewise that through his compassion he comes to our help when he sees us in despair. Instead, were we to live with him, he would be happy to give to all of our gestures the perfect and powerful beauty of his cooperation.

Call upon heaven, yearn for it; breathe heaven's luminous spirit in and out. Breathing exercises recommend the emptying of our lungs completely before filling them with pure air. First, get rid of everything that is self. I do not mean of everything that is earth, because earth and creatures are works of God and contain the reflections of God.

THE HEALINGS OF CHRIST

What I mean is: get rid of the covetousness, possessiveness, cupidity, and vital miserliness that corrupts everything. Then you will find yourselves filled with eternal plenitudes; and everything in us that was destined to death will be returned to life, just as it happened in the case of the young boy of Nain.

Where is Christ?

HOW MANY restless minds are asking the same question these days? Is this thaumaturgist or this thinker the Master, the one who is to come? In the educated and circumspect manner that is his, John the Baptist, the greatest among men, cross-examines mankind knowing full well that a material miracle does not always prove the spiritual legitimacy of the miracle-worker. Yet, the answer of Jesus is a simple one that grants full probative value to the facts as they are.

Why? It is merely because the simplicity of Jesus sees far beyond the critical sense of any psychologist, whereas ordinary man's ignorance remains a partial, superficial, negative simplicity that does not go beyond rational understanding. The simplicity of the disciple, on the other hand, leaves behind it the judiciary of the intellect.

Whoever scorns cerebral pursuits, and various other kinds of human endeavor generally, thereby proves that he has not yet experienced its consuming interest. Those who take their first step on the spiritual paths have a tendency to consider intellectuals, laboratory researchers, and even conscientious observers of moral and religious rules with disdain. Through a whole series of profound essays, Baron Seillière, a serious writer, when calling our attention to the

Reception of Grace

ravages caused by the lack of discipline in one's emotions during the 18th and 19th centuries, accustoms us to link the terms romanticism and mysticism. And, as his commentators do not draw attention to this confusion, the public only falls deeper into the ancient error that misconstrues a mystic as an impulsive person or imaginative dreamer. Yet there is no true mysticism without asceticism or without rigorously following a rule.

Man is not a body; man is not a spirit; man is not a soul. He is a mixture of these three substances, or rather a combination of same. He is a unique substance that does not resemble the matrix-substances, and yet that could not exist without the participation of the three. Any analysis is but an artifice to understand the real by dissociating it; and everything relating to Christ is reality, is life. Do not, then, consider the words in the gospels as mere expressions of facts, or as expressions of sentiments and of ideas, but as realities, as living things, as living beings.

That is why Jesus answers the envoys of the Baptist: "Go and tell John what you have witnessed and heard." These messengers must have acquired at the school of their master (or rather, found again) this sense of the real, this immediate grip of life particular to each fact and to each being, from which we receive the germ before coming down into the cycles of lives, but whose plenitude we will possess only after having trodden all paths and after having reintegrated the kingdom of the Absolute.

In order to receive a ray from the eternal light (whose certain tabernacle is found within each creature and each circumstance), we must have acquired and attained that certain attitude which is both discreet and open-hearted, that survey over all beings, cleansed of any selfish nebulosity; we must have attained comprehension born out of experience, one that is more than indulgence, as it is fraternal and human, also humble and full of dignity. Whatever you may find regarding such scientific states of mind in the books of Claude Bernard, Henri Poincare, and Duhem, apply it to all states of the human mind, and you will comprehend what your behavior in life should be. To get rid of idiosyncrasies is a difficult task; we constantly observe men of high standing closing themselves within four walls—and the worst of it is that they do not know how enclosed they are. Take St Thomas Aquinas, the angelic doctor. He has a unique mind, but does not move away from the Aristotelian platform. Take Napoleon I, prototype of the instruments from the invisible, for whom nothing mattered but cold-reasoning, will-power, and the most mundane and tangible of facts. The religious commentators of the gospel find within it, according to their mental attitude, nothing more than moral maxims or dogmatic theses. Anyone who draws an unusual adaptation from the gospel they regard as an occultist, theosophist, or visionary.

Such is the prestigious power of "sorceress" intelligence. Of course, her role as interpreter of life remains indispensable and important; but she is not satisfied with it. Little by little, through the apparent satisfactions she offers to our imperious need for immediate certitudes, she causes life—sole reality—to disappear behind the images she has helped us to erect. The attitude of the intellectualist resembles that of an engineer who would disregard the reality of the locomotive in favor of lending credence only to his working-drawing and equations.

Truth be told, essential life reflects itself in various mirrors: the mirror of logical thought, the mirror of esthetic

Reception of Grace

sensitivity, the mirror of moral character, the mirror of physical sensitivity. Moreover, these various primary images are in turn dissociated by the innumerable facets of these large lenses into innumerable reflections.

The error of various occultisms was not that they believed in the preeminence of hyperphysical facts over conscious concepts, but that they looked for these primordial facts by starting with matter. The gospel, however, brings us face to face with these facts themselves, introducing us to the kingdom of God, the dwelling place of the Word, where everything pulsates with the most real life. It presents us with the phenomena of this central and permanent world as the principles of our metaphysics, our theologies, our morals, and our sciences. It acclimatizes us to divine Unity through the search for our personal unity. In short, the gospel brings us to God from the center, whereas occultism leads us to him from the outside, and at great risk!

Let us ponder these points in order to be able to answer the accusation made against us of having assembled bits and pieces of heterogeneous doctrines and clothed them as harlequins. For example, although St Françoise Romaine, St Hildegard, the Venerable Anne Catherine Emmerich, and others have copiously described some corners of the invisible to us, never have I stated anywhere that because of this they were occultists or theosophists. Or again, although St Joseph de Cupertino realized many more phenomena than the most illustrious mediums have done, never have I stated that he was a spiritualist (knowing full well, as I do, that any temporal fact may be due to a thousand diverse spiritual causes). Theologians who criticize us should use the same impartial measures. True, we do not propel our interlocutors to the confessional by force, but that does not mean we are

THE HEALINGS OF CHRIST

Protestants. When we recommend an ascetic discipline, or having recourse to the Virgin, we are all too often catalogued as a special brand of Catholics.

The older you become, the more you will recognize how rare are common sense, impartiality, and independence. Thus, Jesus recommends that we judge not, that we should strive to see things by setting all our likes and dislikes aside, to appreciate them regardless of our interests, to compare them without yielding to our passions. This is extremely difficult to do, but merits all our efforts to that end.

Let us attempt to pierce all fogs, which is the paramount essence found in all the exhortations of Christ. Be mindful also how his answer is always directed to our five senses, our memory, our logic, and our judgment, as when he says: "Look, and go back to your master (the heart) to tell him what you have seen."

And, if you will forgive me for trying to save you from taking many a false step, may your progress towards the liberty of the spirit not let you fall into ridiculous pride. Meditate upon Jesus of Nazareth. There he is, pressed by a few hundred cripples and unfortunates shrieking under the burning sun, amid the flies, the dust, and the stench of the crowd. To heal the sick is not as easily done as to tell your chauffeur: "drive me to the Boulevard des Capucines." No matter how great Christ was, he still had to take under consideration each of these unfortunate people, see his past, from his present filthy physical condition back to his deep moral corruption, which commenced in a very far and distant past. No matter how powerful Christ was, it still was necessary for his saving gesture, for his miraculous word, to reach down to the unknown centers of the cripple and to prevail over their farthest eventual results, both visible and

Reception of Grace

invisible. It is not difficult for the disciple to heal someone; all he has to do is shoulder some inconveniences, then ask heaven, and let heaven take it in hand. But Jesus is both Man and God, donor and implorer. What tension, what unimaginable activity he was under!

In spite of all this fracas, he welcomes the messengers of the Baptist quietly, greets them with gentle words, and goes about his business. Let nothing trouble you. You too, do your job; respond to everyone, not more than is necessary, but as it should be; keep your peaceful serenity, that presence because of which a host of creatures already call you blessed. And, little by little, all these problems we are talking about together will be resolved with total and perfect certainty.

Driving Forces

Let us ponder awhile the modes that Jesus himself enumerates from his redemptive works. To the messengers from John, he cites the blind, the cripple, the lepers, the deaf, the dead, and the ignorant whom he heals; and he proclaims as the center of this star the happiness of those who will accept his Word. Before being sent into the world, man in fact receives from the Father six sparks that his future lives will increase, and that may be designated thus:

1. The faculty of perceiving the forms of all creatures.

2. The faculty to act, to work in the world in which we find ourselves, which amounts to the march of the self along the road upon which the Father places it.

3. The organic faculty by which our vital functions are being equilibrated and give us triple health.

THE HEALINGS OF CHRIST

4. The faculty to understand the language of all creatures, which means, as far as this earth is concerned, the ensemble of all our mental faculties.

5. The creative faculty through which we develop and embellish life, and everything around us: a power as different from plain vital activity as charity differs from selfishness.

6. The faculty, lastly, to be born to a new life, to receive the regenerative energies capable of creating us a second time in the Absolute (these energies having been created primordially in the Relative). The plenary reception of the living truths of the gospel into our soul, into our spirit, and into our body, determines this rebirth.

These six faculties have a correspondence in sets of two. The first and the sixth belong to the light, more particularly to the Holy Spirit. The second and fifth go together, because, not being able to walk (as in the case of cripples) is, in the invisible of the Word, not living; they belong, that is, more particularly to the Son, who is the way and the life. The third and fourth belong to the Father and are closely bound, because physiological corruption at its maximum brings in its wake intellectual incapacity.

Yet, each of these driving forces of the human being is given to him by a sun, of which there are in fact seven in the universe, not just one. The one that gives us light is the yellow one; but there are six others, corresponding approximately to each of the colors of the prism. They too are coupled in space to the centers or foci of three cosmic ellipses, the outlines of which will remain unknown for a long time

Reception of Grace

still. All the other stars our astronomers have classified are those whose light is visible to our eye. But many other worlds exist, worlds just as real as our earth—some denser, others less dense, each having influence one upon the other, almost all of which are inhabited and have received or are about to receive the visit of the redemptive Word.

The two suns closest to us are our visible yellow sun and the one the Hindus call the black sun, or the sun of the dead. This latter has as much influence upon our terrestrial earth as does that of the visible sun. Actually, some disciples can discern this sun at certain hours. For our eyes to acquire this sensitivity, all we need have is resignation during our test periods and to love our fellowmen.

These few notions can hardly be of use in our daily life, and we would unfailingly err were we to utilize them by ourselves. Yet they nourish our hope and furnish the fulcrum to humility. At a time when most of our happily endowed brothers wear themselves out to conquer some inaccessible treasure, it is indispensable for us to repeat, on any and all occasions, that the only domains where a Christian has the right to deploy his powers, and the right to spend them until death, are fighting against his own faults, relinquishing his wealth (this one especially), his likes and dislikes, and even denying his right to happiness as an offerings to his brothers.

We too should, as our Master did, save the maimed, the crippled, the blind, the sick, the ignorant, and the dead. It is possible because on another occasion he told us that we would perform greater miracles than his. Notwithstanding, we must not stop there. Thanks to God, we are able to perceive some of our faults. Let us acknowledge that we only see the lesser ones. Charity will sharpen our glance, yet it

THE HEALINGS OF CHRIST

must be a charity that extends to all creatures, all objects, all states of soul or spirit, all events—just as it applies to physical misery.

You who bear in your heart the wound of universal suffering, ask yourself if that suffering will ever detach itself from humanity—and this is your answer: suffering will remain as long as one man can enjoy life without worrying whether his brother is able to enjoy it with him. Understand that fortune, happiness, power, and intelligence are but poisons for the spiritual heart. Not poisons in themselves—poisons only because of the possessiveness they engender in all who have received such formidable treasures. Also, understand this: Jesus did not come to take away the sorrow of the world as a surgeon removes a cancer. No! For he is that misery itself—frightful, lamentable, magnificent. He came to teach us how to cure that frightful cancer. He came, not to operate upon it, but to heal it by the total and profound transformation of our whole being, which takes place when we obey the law, by which I mean when we accept everything in the world and sacrifice ourselves for everything in the world.

The Messengers

SO, LET US NOT complain anymore about living in an epoch so closely resembling that of Christ. Bad humor and criticism do not rebuild, they can only destroy. Anything, no matter how frightful or cruel, contains a light; seek for the spark instead of fretting and fuming about the dirty ashes. If we cannot help noticing the faults of our times, of our contemporaries, politicians, artists, or scientists, let us at least try not to broadcast them. Those people, no matter

Reception of Grace

how cynical, hard, and devoid of elegance or culture they may be, are still instruments. God leads them, though they believe themselves free. And if God permits their ugliness to give offense to the day, it is because our so-called perfections are still too puny, and their meager radiations permit the deleterious germs existing in such low-lands to subsist.

Take heed. In the immense fields of Creation, in which villages are planetary systems, rivers are oceans of fire, and our world but a fruit rolling upon the roadway, you will always find a crowd. There one finds the Precursor and his messengers; there one always finds Jesus. Hence, taking this scale in consideration, what do the tiny convulsions of our contemporaries amount to? So, you will say, "What about our miserable efforts?" Do not be misled regarding these miserable efforts, for even if they be dust they become formidable if we act as if Jesus were working them through us.

Within us, there also is a noisy crowd, cynical and vulgar; therein, also, in some empty chamber of our spirit, is the Precursor and his messengers. But it is when the messengers depart from the enclosure of our conscience that Jesus rises and speaks. Make it possible, then, for these messengers to depart from you.

A Cause of Fall

IT IS OUR contemporaries' misfortune that they hardly ever want to listen to the supernatural voice.

The consequences resulting from human opinions are as grave as the gravity of the objects to which they relate. This is an obvious enough remark regarding ordinary events that nearly always belong to the natural order of things (the only order usually accepted as real), but it is still more true regarding spiritual things, particularly regarding the judgments one passes upon Jesus.

I am thinking at the moment about what the press has written concerning a play called *Jesus of Nazareth*, recently staged at the Odeon. Critics, at times, write a great deal of nonsense, but criticism far surpasses the measure when the subject matter lies beyond their ken. We often mock politicians and café strategists, but when the same anemic brains discourse upon religious subjects that are infinitely more complex and farther removed from the mental habits of the crowd, everyone thinks it quite natural for them to do so. Freedom of self-examination is excellent, if exercised only by competent and mature people, and on condition, of course, that they be impartial. Today it is mainly used as a smokescreen for incompetency. Renan cut a figure as an initiator to the so-called "broad-minded" people of yesterday, just as Anatole France does to those of his era.

"We are too intelligent to believe," they claim. To be intelligent, according to them, means to accept only what their reason or their five senses can apprehend. But if that were the case, intelligence would stand subject to the refinement of these senses or to the freedom of this reason—hence it would have free play, but in very restricted limits, alas! Were they to admit that religious questions are beyond their understanding, then, of course, they would prove their intelligence to be free from prejudices. But on the contrary, they clinch the matter and speak out against anything beyond their ken. This attitude is hardly scientific (and this is a kind way of putting it).

Since they do not want to change, they are incurable. But in order the better to excuse them, let us remember that they are partially blind: their eyes are sensitive only to phys-

Reception of Grace

ical light, and their conscience only to mental light. They are, however, responsible for their blindness, because one way or another providence always informs them about the existence of a sun other than that of intelligence, and because they refuse to examine this information thoroughly. They forget that one cannot progress except by surpassing one's own limitations, even if only by a hair's-breath. An independent and healthy mind discerns limitations, and because of its avowal of them becomes capable of a renewal of grace, thanks to which it will be able to grow. To be reborn, one must accept to die.

One of the most dastardly utopias of the thinking man is his stubborn insistence on erecting systems for himself. To build a house, one needs stones or bricks, materials that are palpable, measurable, and precise; to erect a system, besides ideas, one needs words, which most often are none too precise. The marvel is that with such limited materials, one nonetheless does sometimes successfully erect a beautiful edifice. But regardless whether the architect be Heraclitus or Aristotle, Thomas Aquinas or Duns Scotus, Descartes or Spinoza, Kant or Bergson, none successfully comprehend the entire universe comprised in their edifice.

An analogous powerlessness is evident in sociology. When used by different writers, identical words may have totally opposite significance. Does not the Marxist materialism of Lenin and the juridical spiritualism of Woodrow Wilson (to name but two people who have passed on) claim the same ends? Do they not speak of justice, universal happiness, and peace?

In literature (to choose the most popular of art forms, and to cite only the dead), whether we read Maurice Barres or Marcel Proust, do we not notice that the one disfigures

THE HEALINGS OF CHRIST

the great entities he celebrates, considering them only by their psychological surface and not by their divine center; and that the other, attracted by the abnormal, gives us his astonishing analyses of sensibility only as marginal notes of an extremely intelligent spectator, but neglects to compose them with a view of a practical application?

In the scientific field, Einstein, as far as the layman can understand, only gives us old truths known since before the Deluge. Do we need integral calculus to understand that an infinite quantity will always remain infinite, in spite of the quantity that we take from it? Freud takes a lot of trouble to explain what uneducated old women know quite well. Bergson calls upon biology in order to teach us that intuition can illuminate us. William James, meanwhile, obstinately fails to distinguish between what is marvelous and what is divine.

Here I call a halt, for would not each and every branch of human endeavor give rise to similar remarks?

Facts, sensations, and ideas are but surface points, points of contact, not centers; that is what we should accept first. Moreover, to a thoughtful being, is not powerlessness to account for a truth the sign of a lacuna in one's conception?

Of course, all these hard workers, these elite intelligences, apply themselves towards one of the external facets of the problems they want to solve: whether the physical facet (phenomena, economy, administration, sensitivity, esthetics, and rites), the intellectual facet, or the emotive facet. Some do not accept the reality of a living God. Yet all know very well that intellectual comprehension is not the real comprehension, for which latter many preparations must be made. One must:

Reception of Grace

accept the sense perceptible world as real;
accept the world of collective entities (race, country, religion) as real;
accept the world of esthetic concepts as real;
accept the abstract world of laws and metaphysics as real;
accept the world of feelings as real;
accept the world of imagination as real; and grant to this epithet the qualities of organicity and life that, for instance, the human animal possesses.

One must accept all these things because everything exists at the same time both in and beyond us; and everything is organic. A perception, an emotion, an idea, a volition are neither psycho-chemical results of cellular reactions nor contacts of wave-lengths: they are encounters between individual beings; they are dramas, combats, marriages, births, and deaths. Someone will retort: anthropomorphism! But why should anthropomorphism be found all along the course of centuries and under all latitudes, were it not the terrestrial expression of a cosmic truth?

In short, psychological activity as a whole tends to engender comprehensions and notions to the solidity of which intelligence, emotivity, and sensitivity concur—but merely as auxiliaries. The childbirth known as certainty needs a father and a mother; why need we invent pseudonyms for them, since their progenitors are called the eternal light and the love of perfection?

Those, then, who do not admit that Jesus is God, whether they consider him in the pantheistic manner, or hold this title to be an entitlement of the Church (or for other reasons that it seems unseemly to repeat), Jesus declares them unfor-

THE HEALINGS OF CHRIST

tunate rather than guilty. Firstly, unfortunate, because they are heading for the wrong road and incomprehensible suffering; secondly, a little guilty, because they could really see things clearly if they admitted they were not infallible.

The apparition of light is always salvific. It immediately brings salvation to the minority who, as soon as they perceive it, accept it; then, little by little, it saves the innumerable majority, who refused it at first. This refusal, in fact, pushes the unbelievers back into a darker night, in the midst of which they struggle to emerge into a day that they still reject, but with less violence. Thus, oscillating from shadows to brighter and brighter light, at the end of a certain number of cycles, which come in six or in multiples of six, the blind surrender and the light heals them.

The return of these prodigal children doubtless procures a great joy to the Father and his angels. But these erring ones are not yet happy, because they still have to exhaust repentance and make some amends for the wrongs their vagrancies have sown throughout the world. He only has beatitude who, through a superhuman effort of humility, accepts Christ as soon as he perceives him. For (and this is the great mystery of Jesus Christ's friendship) the individual, while enjoying full plenitude of his own psychological conscience, may live at one and the same time on earth and in heaven. The roots of the tree toil in the obscurity of the soil, among stones and vermin; the leaves on the branches of the tree labor in light and air. Now, the branches and the roots belong to the same tree, and the particles that suffered in darkness slowly ascend towards the sun. Then, during the autumn, the leaves fall and slowly disintegrate, forming the nourishing humus from which the roots reabsorb the essence during the winter. So it is, but inversely, for the disciple. He is a tree whose roots rise into the infinite realm of heaven, and who gives to the earth its marvelous flowers and its miraculous fruits. He lives in total joy, since he nourishes himself above—or through his center—on the beatitudes of love; and below, he offers to matter what he brings from heaven, through the equally blessed sacrifices of that same love.

Preaching the Word

AFTER HAVING sent back to their master the disciples of John the Baptist (who had come to interrogate him on behalf of the prince of repentance), Jesus, addressing himself to the crowd, exclaims justifiably: "Blessed is the man who does not lose confidence in me!"

Many scientists claim to recognize that life in everything; this, however, is but to recognize the Word only within the circle of the sense-perceptible. Many artists and poets sing or paint the beauties of universal harmony; this, however, is but to recognize the Word in the sphere of animic emotions. Many philosophers discover a living organization in the field of abstract laws; this, however, is but to recognize the Word in the frozen sky of metaphysics. Physico-chemical reactions, waves and vibrations of cosmic energies, emanations and concepts, subjectivisms and pantheisms—all are nothing but shadows projected upon various screens by the divine Being who travels throughout the world.

Those who recognize Jesus Christ as the only Son of God, made flesh and resurrected, come out of darkness and enter into the real.

Many Christians, however, only profess such a belief either because of their training or through obedience. Others, who are more conscientious, have probed into a system of moral proofs or logical demonstrations in favor of this truth. Finally, others, feeling that truth is truth only when it expresses itself through life, preoccupy themselves with giving life to this indispensable truth by mixing it with their thoughts, their feelings, their words, and especially their actions. These are the disciples, servants, and friends of Jesus.

When I state that those who do not accept this truth belong to the Antichrist, I am not anathematizing them. I simply classify them. They are to be pitied rather than condemned; they should be enlightened, not shunned.

Religion is a living entity. It is that part of life where it is most intense. Here the act is more important than the thought, fervor more important than the rule. Has St Augustine not said: "Love first, and then do as you will"? But we must love through actions, and not through intentions only.

The great leaders of men utilize diverse methods to attract and hold the crowds. Some arrive at that end by imposing a system of rules and precise disciplines. Others maintain their hold by directing opinions through clever publicity campaigns. But there are yet others (and these are the true apostles) who guide and convert through the living attraction of example. If you are clever dialecticians, merely erudite and eloquent, the unbelievers you convert will become so through their intellect and in their intelligence. But to become true disciples, they will sooner or later have to make the effort of leaving the intellectual domain in order to enter the kingdom of the heart. Be authoritarian, and the results will be even more precarious and superficial.

But if you carry in your heart the ardent conviction that

Reception of Grace

you are nothing, possess nothing, can do nothing, and that Jesus is everything and can do all things, and if you continue living normally among people of your own station, being helpful to all, indulgent and anticipating the needs of the poor, even to giving more than is asked of you—then doubtless among your auditors there will be many who will exploit and make fun of you. But the day their nastiness leaves you totally indifferent, you will not have to receive them anymore. As to the others, without your having delivered them a sermon, they will wonder why you act in such a way, and of their own accord they will come to you, and your answer will germinate within them. You will have grafted a wild-stock upon the eternal Vine. You will have taught your brothers in the knowledge of the Word.

We cannot repeat often enough that fulfilling the gospel grants everything—health, opportunity, money, knowledge, eloquence—when these material things are useful to some of our brothers or even when we have need of them. In the latter case, be it well understood that we have not performed the gestures of a disciple in the hope of personal recompense. The first condition for being heard by heaven is selflessness.

Often, erudite and clever unbelievers have been confounded by a simple, ignorant but authentic disciple enlightened by his Master. Moreover, in prevision of the innumerable attacks Christic truth is called to bear during the current century, heaven has decreed that such a bewilderment of human knowledge by mystical simplicity would be increased. The application of a celebrated expression is meant here: "When you shall be called before the tribunals, do not worry what answer you are to give."

This promise was made to us. It is up to us to make ourselves capable of receiving such inspiration from the Holy Spirit. Everything has been offered us. All we need do is consecrate our entire forces to prepare in our hearts as worthy a tabernacle as we can for these supernatural gifts.

It is imprudent to speak of Christ, Son of God, without discretion. For without such discretion, we can provoke mocking, we can cause others to do evil just as if we gave a baby too copious a feeding. We can cause scandal if we do not offer our interlocutor the example of a conduct perfectly worthy of the ideal we affirm. Neither should we seem fearful. Genuine preaching is our lived existence. If our actions provoke questions, answer with calm, with measure, without acrimony or haughtiness.

The joy Jesus grants those who recognize him is not only in the future, it is in the present too. Just as the little misfortunes of life do not check the enthusiasm of the artist, the serenity of the philosopher, or the force of movers and shakers dedicated to some great purpose, so our commerce with Jesus puts back into their true place (a very small place) all these inconveniences, affronts, and wounds that make so many of our contemporaries boil with anger. And this deep, living peace does not resemble the indifference and impassibility of the Stoic.

The Precursor

IT IS OF COURSE human to try to find around us someone to lean upon, a guide for our uncertainties. Before Christ, men had always grouped themselves behind supermen; and after Christ, this lack of faith has maintained them in the same fearful dependency. We moderns are no better. In fact, there are also many learned people who assert the need

Reception of Grace

for visible guides, that we are quite excusable for sticking to intermediaries. On the other hand, our blundering mind, incoherence, anemic enthusiasms, inconstancy, suggestibility—alas! all these make us incapable of following the path of the gospel, which is too simple for our complication, too narrow for our vacillating steps. Being what we are, we need analysts, commentators, who little by little clarify our analytical intelligence. We think we need robust guides to invent artificial exercises to give us back our plumb line. We think we need imperfect examples because we imagine the example of Christ to be too perfect for us.

We resemble the budding swimmer who would like to go through the swimming motions on land. One has to take the step to enter into the kingdom under the immediate tutelage of Jesus. We hardly dare jump across the ditch. Though nothing is easier, we dare not.

As children of nature, we are only willing to listen to other children of nature, older no doubt, but children of nature all the same. That is why, having compassion for this puerile weakness, Jesus raises up before him a precursor.

What is this man? Not an illuminati, not a stump-orator like so many others who draw crowds by pandering to their grudges, at the whim of passions, like reeds bending in all directions with the wind. Neither is he powerful in the temporal sense. But he is a seer in the spiritual sense, a prophet, a man guided by the Spirit. He is more than a prophet whose mission remains local and accidental—he is an envoy whose mission is universal and perpetual. In short, "the greatest of all those born of women."

We have already looked at this superhuman figure whose grandeur has struck the greatest of ecclesiastical savants with admiration. According to Chrysostomus, the Baptist would not have needed any human master; because, as both St Ambrose and Origen affirm, from the time of the Visitation he had full use of all his faculties; he was a prophet-born according to St Paulinus and the Abbé Gueric-d'Igny. The renowned Gerson states that he received the place vacated by Lucifer, so that according to tradition he sits at the left of Christ, at whose right Mary is seated. Lastly, St Augustine declares that he is so lofty that anyone loftier would be God.

In any case, he is "more than a prophet," because he has seen all truth; he is the herald of the New Law. Up to his time, the orb of nature was closed. Supreme flower of the supreme efforts of men, he has blossomed at the first sight of his Master on the way to this earth; he is the necessary premise for the acceptance of heaven; he is the indicator of the road; he bathes our tired eyes so that the brilliance of the rising sun will not close them; through him, the veil of the beyond has been raised for us.

The Baptist, hence, is only a man, but he is unique. And if we read the gospels under the light of eternity, the Baptist appears to us as a man who has experienced everything, accomplished all works, borne all trials, conquered all monsters, deciphered all enigmas, ascended all summits.

He is greater than Moses or Solomon, greater than Fo-Hi or Lao-Tze, than Krishna or Buddha, than Zoroaster, Odin, or Muhammad—this is what, if we are Christians, faith in Jesus orders us to believe. I am aware that this opinion is contrary to the critics, contrary to all the testimonies of history invoked by rationalism, contrary to common reasoning. Fine. But it is the truth. Let us, in fact, interrogate this selfsame historical science invoked by rationalism: do we not notice that behind all of those celebrated people, those leaders of men, those reformers, there have always

Reception of Grace

been secret inspirers and anonymous advisors who directed them while furnishing them the necessary means for their impact and influence? In the world, everything goes by pairs. Does not Christ himself always relate or couple himself with his celestial Father? Does not John the Baptist proclaim the one who is to come after him as one whose shoelace he is not worthy to untie?

So, the greater the glory, the less it is known. John the Baptist, the greatest among men, is one of the least known; and these very little ones in the kingdom of heaven, those whom Christ declares to be greater than the Precursor, are, totally unknown. You will object: Christ, whom you call the greatest, the loftiest, has been celebrated for centuries, is well known, since hundreds upon hundreds of scholars and thinkers have studied and are still studying his doctrine and his history. I grant that Christ seems well-known and seems to enjoy the greatest renown possible, but it is purely an exterior knowledge—a human celebrity in reality. Just as his physical personality remained obscure during most of his lifetime, so does his spiritual personality remain, since his death, and will remain till the end of the world, just as misunderstood and obscure. That is because this personality is incomprehensible to man in spite of all acumen of scholarly minds or all of the love of saints. Between these disciples, no matter how admirable or venerable they are, and their Master, an abyss always separates their relative from his absolute. No matter how beautiful or pure they are, they still stand as creatures before the Creator. And we will never comprehend more than an infinitesimal image of the Word, of Christ, of Jesus. Let us meditate upon these extraordinary ideas. They may not furnish us with numerous and practical applications, but they acquaint us with

THE HEALINGS OF CHRIST

the spirit of the gospel that is always at the antipodes to the spirit of humanism.

The kingdom of heaven, universe of infinite grandeur, is called Reality. Nature, tiny mirror where one sees the reflection of the innumerable hosts and of the immense firmament, site of finite grandeur, reflects the image of heaven while inverting its forms. That occurs within the order of concepts just as it does in the moral order, as well as in the order of substances. Thus, the powerful, the scholars, and those famous according to nature are small, ignorant, and weak according to God. The gospel gives abundant illustrations of this truth. So our Precursor will be great before God in proportion to his insignificance before men; he will diminish in measure as his Master increases; he will accomplish in all the modes of activity this work of turn-back to the principles, this spiritual integration that in moral terms is called repentance and penance.

Let us clearly understand this. God has given us the seed of liberty; hence he interdicts himself from doing anything for us unless we of our own free will express our free desire to be helped by him. This expression is the whole of asceticism: repentance, remorse, penance, renunciations, sacrifices, resignation. Since all creatures have sinned, all creatures have to repent. Just so, since all is alive, the Precursor gives to all creatures a lesson and sets the example.

His singular dignity is that wherever his Master wants to descend, he goes first and clears the way for him. But we are not talking about speeches here; we are talking about real work, spiritual fatigue that is far more exhausting than bodily fatigue. Upon a certain world, the world of Christ to be precise, states of soul—anxiety, solicitude, compassion, exhortation, repentance, and prayer—are the acts and for-

Reception of Grace

mal works of our spirit. This is the labor of the Baptist. And he fulfills it on all planes: in the lower realms as well as in the heart of man; in the invisible worlds as well as upon this earth. For such a formidable effort, he has to be the greatest of the children of men.

Penitence

The Precursor, angel of repentance and of penitence, is the hero of those secret tragedies, of those intimate cataclysms that in the inner being of converts devastate and carry everything away with them, leaving bare the rock of selfishness, of pride, and of self-esteem. Then this rock still has to be shattered by the explosives of remorse and total contrition.

There are two types of penance to which we may be subjected: the penance we impose upon ourselves according to the remorse that a subtle ray of divine pity kindles in our heart; and the harder penance that heaven imposes on us to purify the innermost recesses of our moral person. Thus, John preached repentance to the crowds, reserving for himself the practice of merciless austerities.

Recognizing the evil we commit is difficult for our human nature, and makes it uncomfortable; insensitivity combines here with blindness, and pride with weakness.

There is an acclimatization of our conscience to evil; there is in evil a force of corruption that renders our return to spiritual health more and more difficult, the more we dither. Very rarely do we really and deliberately want to be bad; rather, more often than not, we do not want to be better. We have no concept of what redemption is, or what the descent of the Word was, or of the universality and the individuality of its effects.

THE HEALINGS OF CHRIST

We who feel loathe to deprive ourselves of the smallest comfort, just imagine what must have been the infinite privations, the innumerable diminishments that the Word imposed upon himself all during the immense voyage of his descent to earth! Where is the genius capable of conceiving such a rosary of sacrifices? And after reaching the earth, Jesus Christ did not work or suffer merely for the rank and file of his contemporaries, or for the masses of future generations. No, he suffers still for each individual, one and all, for each personally. Each of his pains "points its finger" at us. Jesus had foreseen each of our wrongdoings and had done something so that out of each of our iniquities good may result. And each of our feelings or actions, each of our thoughts or willful decisions, can be, at our choice, a new wound for him, or a collaboration in his universal work.

Hence, we must maintain a feeling of remorse for all our faults, not because of the painful consequences they may have for us, but because they hurt others and make our Lord and Friend suffer in his spiritual body and in his most compassionate, loving heart.

Finally, we must repent, both in our heads and in our hearts, through incentives of thinking and of feeling.

As far as the former are concerned, any misbehavior or fault is a disobedience; to disobey means we believe ourselves wiser than God, or we do not know how to govern ourselves. This signifies that we voluntarily disarrange the designs of God, that we circumscribe them, that we place ourselves beyond their influence. Moreover, sooner or later we lessen ourselves, weaken ourselves, since in this way we introduce within ourselves the germs of corruption, and our radiation upon others is thereby obscured.

After repentance comes expiation: whether it be that

Reception of Grace

which we self-impose by contriving ways of atoning for the harm we have done others; that of subjecting ourselves to a rigorous discipline to conquer our faults; that which God imposes upon us as expiation through adversities, material tests, illnesses, persecutions, and reverses; or, lastly, that of the inner turmoils of aridity, sadness, temptations, and nights of the soul.

Theoretically, this is what we may learn regarding the inner regime of penitence: more subtle than the former tests, it demands fervor first of all. The disciple must be consumed with the desire for God, must burn inwardly. Only the ardor of his love will make of him a true disciple, by making him capable, through the number and intensity of his sufferings, of traveling in a few years the road that the lukewarm take centuries to achieve. I say centuries because, whether we accept the theory of rebirths, whether we hold to the theory of purgatory, whether time be not the same on this earth as it is upon other worlds, the purification of the heart is still an infinitely complex work.

For material ordeals to bear their full fruits, it is enough to endure them, but with resignation, with calm, and, if possible, with joy! The "soldiers of Christ" are the elite disciples who, not satisfied with bearing what comes to them, request a share beyond their power of suffering, so as to surpass the possible. These are the ones who, not content with suffering for their own sake, ask to suffer in the stead of their brothers whom it will please Christ to solace. The heart of these beings is aflame with incandescent and dazzling light. May our whole desire be to emulate them!

Our innermost tests arrive, just like the preceding ones, independently of our will. It is God who sends them to us. They consist of diverse states of disgust, of obstacles that

THE HEALINGS OF CHRIST

prevent our being united with God through prayer or moral achievements. These are involuntary distractions, scruples, our apparent powerlessness to love God and to do good to others; they are sadness and discouragement due to the evil in us; bitterness of feeling isolated; doubt regarding the phenomena of our inner life or our salvation, or regarding primary truths, such as the existence of God and his kindness; certitude of being lost; frightful hunger for God; involuntary antipathy towards God. Besides these, come the different temptations God permits the adversary to present to us.

These punishments are the glorious prerogative of the "violent." If I go along my merry little way in the belief that all the time I need lies before me, that divine patience will settle all things, that what I do not achieve now I will do later, that perhaps someone else will do it for me, that my actions have little importance, that I am weary, that others work less than I do—this is patent lukewarmness, sheer laxity. To be violent means to understand that the present minute is the only minute that belongs to us, that from it depends our whole future, that time wasted can never be regained, that it is cowardly to let anyone else do the work we were supposed to do, that our slightest gesture (if we incorporate God into it) is given a greater value, that only the flesh and nature are lazy, but the élan of pure love never feels fatigue; that no one else may fulfill what is our assigned task, and finally, that no other consideration should exist when we are faced with the slightest chance of lessening the dolor of the world and the weariness of Jesus. Violence is the reification of all of these notions into facts.

No matter how degrading it was, the temptation that has been repulsed does not soil the heart. Soiling only begins with the acceptance. God does not in any case permit the

Reception of Grace

devil to torment us except when he knows we are strong enough to withstand his attacks.

As to the frightful states of soul enumerated above, let us look at them from the standpoint of heaven. We will then clearly gauge the character of the true disciple. Just as great intelligences are modest, so does it seem to the heroes of charity that they do but little for others. The love of Christ and of his fellowmen is so deeply ingrained into the moral person of the true disciple that he almost feels devoid of that quality. Here again extremes meet: the saint ignores his beauty as much as the instinctive criminal ignores his wickedness. When the frozen clouds of the mystical night will descend upon you, remember that one loves God by the sole fact of wanting to love him, provided that one affirms this want by doing good works; and that the anguish of not feeling our love for him is the truest love.

Let us be very happy if the sight of our faults causes us as much discomfort as the sight of our neighbor's faults once did. Let us rejoice when we are deprived of the joys of friendships, when insurmountable obstacles cause our projects to fail, when we come to a standstill, when every worldly thing, the arts and sciences we cherished, are become insipid to us. Let us gather calm about us when doubt, discouragement, and despair come, when our mind becomes incapable of concentrating and of following ideas through. That is because God wants us to become totally humble, to belong solely to him, to expect profound and peaceful joy, knowledge, strength, and confidence to come from him alone.

If you are assailed by scruples, make yourself very small, and understand that God is good—far more good than just—and that if you make a mistake through good inten-

THE HEALINGS OF CHRIST

tions, he will not hold your error against you. When everything loses its savor, even kindheartedness, even prayer, even your sacrifices, then make yourself still smaller; and in spite of all, continue to do good, to pray, to deprive yourselves, even were you absolutely convinced it was in vain.

As far as obsession or diabolical possession are concerned, these are not graver tests than others; on the contrary, they seem to be more grave, but it is not so. They are always interposed with the rarest and strongest helps.

Let us recapitulate, if you please, all these observations (upon which hundreds of volumes have been written). I am only giving you the bare essentials, but we might also delve somewhat further.

For example, here is a disciple, who tries his skill at prayer, at being charitable, at fighting against his faults. He is engaged in what the theologians call purgative life. From time to time God sends him help, grants some of his requests. He is one among the average Christians.

If this disciple intensifies his efforts, then all of a sudden, in the habitual desire that draws him ever higher towards God, there enters a sensation of aridity, of bitterness, and also many passing distractions—all of which is penetrated by the anxious desire for the divine Presence. At the same time he feels that the inclinations he had for certain physical works or mental exercises, the yearning he felt towards certain human goals, crumble and fall away. St John of the Cross calls this period the first night of the soul. During this period, one must remain calm and wait, while neglecting no duty.

When this night is over, without having done anything special, we find ourselves endowed with the definite feeling of the divine Presence, but with variations of duration and

Reception of Grace

intensity. According to the disciple's inner attitudes, the union stops there, or else goes much deeper, in which case the disciple passes through the inner purifications mentioned above, those of the second night of St John of the Cross. This union develops further and may even reach ecstasy; the communications with the sense world become more or less intermittent.

However, prior to ecstasy, there occur other phenomena known in Catholic terminology as powers, wounds, stigmata, raptures, visions, revelations, thaumaturgies, etc. Whatever form the phenomenon takes, it always means that the person of the mystic has been captured or is possessed by a divine ray. This capture affects mobility, one or several of the senses, one or several of the mental or psychic faculties—it matters not which. Its characteristics always remain: the impossibility for the disciple to put himself in that state, the probable incomprehensibility of the phenomenon, the effacement of imagination and of intellectual faculties. Hence, very little volition is at work here: the heart limits itself to feeling attached to God, to one's fellowmen, and to greater desire for perfection.

Then, after the regime of ecstasies, the third night can occur, also known as transforming union, the seventh abode, or spiritual marriage. This is the last stage. If one reaches it, it has been through a thousand imperceptible transitions, and it confers startling privileges. Conscious union with God persists even during shabby or profane occupations, as if the disciple were twofold—a kind of deification of his mental and psychic being results from his conversation, or rather from this permanent companionship with God. However, one does not see God: one knows, one feels, one has the certainty of his presence, and understands what he says without any audible sound. The disciple is not lost in God like a drop of water returning to the ocean, as the yogis claim. He has entered the eternal Vine; the wildstock lives from the life of the vine, but is not the vine.

This is where I stop. In reality, the stages of the mystical union are not platforms to be reached by leaps and bounds; everything happens in gradations, the sequence and nature of which vary with each disciple, for each disciple is a world apart. This path is extremely difficult and delicate, full of risks and pitfalls; it requires cloistered solitude. So the Father opens to us laymen, who are not even free to follow a diet, other paths leading to the same goal, and perhaps even higher still.

Let us be quite clear: for a certain part of humanity, God has willed a body of religious knowledge and practice that make up the admirable organism of the Church: theology, liturgy, asceticism, and mysticism form its functions, linked together and dependant on one other. But, just as there can be a theology as true as Thomism, but different, there can be a liturgy, an asceticism, a mysticism other than those of Catholicism, and just as good. The gospel contains both.

The Evolution of Mysticism

To confine ourselves to mysticism, of which there are as many varieties as there are theologies, sciences, and arts, let us expressly specify that Christian mysticism is recognizable by this one sufficient and necessary sign: that the disciple, knowing the divinity of Jesus to be real, finds in him and in him alone the way, the life, and the truth. Of the three great confessions of Christianity (the three parts of the garments of the crucified drawn by lots among the soldiers of Caesar),

Reception of Grace

neither Orthodoxy nor the Protestants have undertaken an in-depth study of mysticism because the followers of the former are, so to speak, pious children, and the "free self-examination" tendency of the latter leads to a cut-and-dried moralism, or to an almost critical rationalism. Even so, in the Protestant Germanic countries let us name, Gilles Gutman, H. Madathanus, Jacob Boehme, Abraham de Frankenberg, J.G. Gichtel, and the later Oetinger; in England, Jeanne Leade and Pordage; in Sweden, Swedenborg—all of whom are mystics since they believed in Christ as the only-begotten Son of God, and they brought their sometimes unusual explorations in certain regions of the kingdom of God to a good end. Their practical method to some degree resembles that followed by the Franciscans.

Catholic mysticism offers the seeker a greater number of systems that, though aiming for the same goal and utilizing the same supports, do vary as to method. This corps of doctrines and works has developed little by little. The apostles and the first disciples were mystics; but, living in the vicinity of the Light who illumined them, entirely absorbed into its soft splendor, bathed in its revivifying warmth, busily engaged in the needs of the present—they were not giving thought to analysis.

Ten or twelve centuries would have to pass before we discuss the stages of the soul's journey to God. It would take volumes and the labor of a whole institute to draw a complete picture of the doctrinal corpus of Catholic mysticism: from the Desert Fathers down to St Thomas Aquinas, and from him to the final doctors such as St Ignatius of Loyola, St Theresa, Rodriguez, St Francis de Sales, Scaramelli, Surin, and many others. Moreover, we who tend towards re-establishing direct contact with the eternal sap of the tree of

THE HEALINGS OF CHRIST

the Cross need a panoramic view of the whole rather than analyses pursued to their nth degree, for we don't have the time to probe into them.

Sufficient unto us is to discern the three main currents within the rich organism of Catholic mysticism:

> The Dominican school, following St Thomas Aquinas, truly seeks to find divine union through prayer and good works, but does so through the utilization of the resources of thought to sanctify study and rejoin the Absolute by means of metaphysics.
>
> The Franciscan school is devout. Here one chooses to become materially poor, and loves Jesus so strongly that one ends by receiving from him spiritual poverty.
>
> The Ignatian school is that of the will. The practitioner of the *Spiritual Exercises* wills. His physical penitences, his studies, his moral disciplines, aim at exalting his will to the highest degree, so that it may become docile to the action of grace.

Here again one meets the three parts of the garments of Jesus. But there is also the seamless robe, woven by the Virgin Mary herself, the threads of which are the ordinary disciples, the most guileless, the closest to the sacred person of the Master. Whatever may be the outer Church into which they were born, they belong to the inner Church.

This is why from time to time one meets in every school a disciple who makes the connection to the central school. For instance, the Dominican St Vincent Ferrier, possessed of a formidable eloquence, founder of doctrines of integrity, whose miracles amaze the crowds, bequeaths to us a perfect rule of mysticism in his *Treatise of Spiritual Life*. Then,

Reception of Grace

among the sons of St Francis, one meets eminent doctors such as Reverend Father Yves and Father Joseph. Also, among the Jesuits, orators such as Bourdaloue and mystics such as the Reverend Fathers Surin, Louis Lallemant, and de Caussade. More generally, and for all its children, each period of the history of the Church offers a great doctor, a great preacher, a great contemplative, and a great thaumaturgist, so that an equilibrium as close to perfect health as the troubled atmosphere of this world will permit will be re-established between all of the organs of this vast body.

But among these various ways, our way seems best suited to our condition. Theory and the outer forms of piety, being reduced to bare essentials, leave us more free time for practical works and inner discipline. However, the revealing statement: "Violence breaks down the doors of heaven," applies to any and all paths, since we can do violence to each form of the self. The Carmelite nun will do violence to the fragility of her body; the Visitation sister will do violence to her will; the Jesuit will have to dominate his own inclinations. But if the disciple of the fourth school—that of the seamless robe—wants to storm the eternal fortress, he will have to be unrelenting to himself, he will subject all tyrannies to his needs, as much as to his passions or his opinions; he will closely observe his way of living and smother immediately everything springing from the dark roots of personality and of selfishness. The greater his ardor of joining the Word consumes him, that much the more autocratic will he be against himself. Such is the school of the Precursor. And Jesus recommends it to us at another time when he exclaims: "If your hand makes you sin, cut it off." I notice that the gospel does not address itself to the indolent or the lukewarm.

THE HEALINGS OF CHRIST

I am well aware that many Christians prefer treating their faults more diplomatically. Thousands of little psychological aids are offered to their tottering will-power, a thousand little tonics given to their cooling zeal. But towards this multitude of mediocre souls agitated only with rather mingy concerns, the Church extends the patience, foresight, and resourcefulness of a most admirable mother. Furthermore, it is God who inspires the spirit of this precautionary education engendered by this tender expression: "Do not break the bruised twig."

Whoever feels in his heart a more ardent flame, however, has the self-imposed duty of choosing the path of the Precursor. Is it not written: "I shall spew the lukewarm from my mouth"? This path, the one of total action, of incessant action, is the shortest and surest, but also the steepest one. To remain on it one must have energy, flexibility, the timeliness of the realist, serenity, a meditative quality, and a contemplative's detachment. But our Christ sees us, he sends us help, and we find ourselves face to face with him (if I may I say so) centuries ahead of the crowd, since time differs on each world—much sooner, in any case, than we would have dared hope. As recompense, he offers us the glorious mission of descending again among the lingering flock, to instill some courage and get them over some rough patches.

This is the individual aspect of the mission of the Precursor. Its collective aspect is its multiplication on a larger scale. The prophets bring spiritual food to a people or to a race. Within the individual, the prophets are their intuitions. I have neither time nor space to follow the multiform activity of providence all along the path of history; but, just as some individuals are indifferent, others more enthusiastic, still others flamboyant with ardor, so there are nations that mark

Reception of Grace

time, others that choose shortcuts. One of these latter is renowned in the epic of Europe's history. Another we see suffering at the moment, without understanding her convulsions. Always and everywhere, heaven sends prophets for daily progress, and at least once in the life of a race, heaven sends the Precursor for the terminal assault. Therefore, just as John the Baptist was Elijah, so the Precursor is always the Precursor, no matter under which guise he appears at the given moment—just as his King, our Savior, is always Christ—our Jesus.

Vigilance

WHEREVER beings are who await the coming of Christ, they have to live under the regime of the Precursor, in prayer and vigilance. To be on watch means to be awake. It also means leading our senses and our powers just as the shepherd leads his flock, bringing our capricious animals back ever and again to the one and only pasture. It also means being a professional trainer, who, like the one who schools inattentive dogs, repeats without impatience a command a thousand times if necessary, with steady calm and constant firmness.

We are, in fact, two within ourselves; or rather, we comprise both one and many ("flocks"). According to pagan, worldly wisdom, one is will, and everything else flocks: the *body*, with its senses and instincts; the *character*, with its passions, habits, vices, and virtues; the *intellect*, with its ideas, concepts, and mental architectures; the *psyche*, with all that the invisible world brings (lights and shadows alike) to the border zone between the unconscious with the conscious.

THE HEALINGS OF CHRIST

But in our Christian wisdom or teachings, besides these four flocks, there is still one more stubborn flock to be lead, the flock of wills, because the center of our being is found in the very core of the will, in the center of our spiritual heart.

So, take the habit of becoming spectators of your own self. When viewing anything, internal or external, let your observatory be the viewpoint of God. Even a seemingly admirable impulse, or the effort expended on behalf of others, gains in purity, spiritual value, and material fruits, when subjected to the touchstone: "Thy will be done and not mine," to which a glance from the Word always responds.

In doing so, do not be afraid of becoming inert or indecisive; you will appear inert to the roughnecks, indecisive to the birdbrains, but your heart will continue to burn while you await the divine response, and your energy, for having deferred a little, will be the more vigorous and lucid as a result. Moreover, is not God always way above, way beyond? Whatever may be the inebriation of an ecstasy, it is nothing but a veil of his splendor unfolded before us by the angels. The words he is willing to let us hear, he brings down to the level of our meager understanding. The true face of God will remain invisible to us and his voice will remain inaudible to us as long as we not have become freemen (new men).

Let us make use of our ears and eyes. We must do so, because it is written: "Let him who has ears, hear." But no matter how pure or how good our intentions may be, never forget that our ears and eyes, like our intelligence, like our emotions, like our will, like our conscience, are but imperfect organic systems incapable of receiving the perfect. You will then know how to enter the desert of the mystical night without anything altering your confidence; you will know how to choose what is the harder and most difficult; you will know that it is when our Friend seems very far away that he stands closest to our side, though under an as yet imperceptible form, because it is so pure, so lofty!

The Gospel and Intelligence

ONE OF THE MOST frequent reproaches directed against the gospel by freethinkers is the so-called condemnation it appears to level against intelligence, energy, and material success.

I believe you are by now convinced that, far from preaching a doctrine of lazy abdication, the gospel preaches, on the contrary, a most persevering and tenuous energy, which we are to apply in our moral life as in our performance of charitable acts. Neither does the gospel condemn the initiatives of the worker in whatever field he works. On the contrary, the Master addresses his reprimands to the timorous agent who buried his talents, while he praises the active agent who made his fructify. Neither does the gospel condemn knowledge or the productive labors of the artist and of the philosopher.

What the gospel does condemn is the use men make of the fruits of their labor. The treasures that men accumulate instead of sharing them with others (after keeping what is essentially needful for their use) is the one thing that prevents the rich from entering the kingdom of heaven. The pride that the successful realization of his first masterpieces engenders in an artist hypnotizes him; it keeps from him possible revitalizations for his genius, hence bars from him the road of eternal beauty. He condemns himself to the rut his temperament drags him into; and no matter how rare

THE HEALINGS OF CHRIST

his temperament or its quality may be—a rut is still a rut. Were the artist humble, were he conscious that his gifts do not confer any meritorious reward and that his tribulations are simply the frame to the "talent" entrusted to him and thus part and parcel of his normal duty, the walls preventing the descent of divine inspiration from reaching him would collapse and he could paint for us, not merely the beauties of the senses, the beauties of nature, the beauties of love, but the perfect and pure beauties of the spirit.

Do understand that the same humble openness of soul, the same deferential aspiration in the face of the mysteries of total knowledge, would also renew the intelligence of laboratory researchers and thinkers, and unleash their intuition.

If you study the lives of great achievers, leaders of peoples or captains of industry, you will see that the causes of their triumphs or failures can be summed up either in the acuity of their vision, or in their blindness; and as well, that their blindness was sustained by a just sense of human weakness, rather than being the consequence of unintelligent pride.

So when the gospel glorifies the poor, the ignorant, the suffering, and those who practice professions that are descried, it is not revolutionary rhetoric: it is because from the very first (no matter what motivates them, and although we may be the guilty ones), weakness and sorrow move the tenderness of the Father, the compassion of the Son, and call the Spirit forth; it is because the heart of the poor is not crushed by a strong-box safe; it is because the heart of the ignorant is not petrified by following some kind of system that although held to be definite, yet is only and always provisional; it is because a suffering heart dematerializes and becomes detached from the prestige of our society; it is because the one upon whom are heaped the

Reception of Grace

contempt of so-called respectable people sighs with invincible hope from the depths of its misery.

As far as we can discern, God's plan concerning our race is to lead it in its entirety, by means of a living knowledge, to a vaster power of beatitude, one much more powerful than the one it enjoyed when it still belonged to the angelic hierarchies. We were then living in the eternal, in the infinite, in the perfect, in the absolute. I can say this at a time when all paradoxes are accepted—but this absolute is not a uniform world. The Eastern sages and our mathematicians err when they consider *Parabrahma* or infinite grandeurs as fixed states or immobile quantities. "There are many mansions in the house of the Father." The house of our Father is not nature; nature is but the domain that surrounds the palace our Lord inhabits. Yes, incessant eternities move in Eternity; measureless spaces criss-cross in Infinitude; innumerable, diverse, and all-total perfections shine forth in Perfection; ever-growing, perfect, and eternal beatitudes sing forth in the limitless beatitude of Love.

Into the furrows of nature the Father, by handfuls, casts the seeds of light that we, in essence, are. All these seeds are different. They may look alike, but none is identical to another. Thus do we fall into a field of prodigious immensity, where each clod of earth is a system of worlds, and each furrow a nebula. Then comes the obscure travail of germination.

First of all, the Sower begins at one end of the field and ends at the other. The Harvester will enter from one end of the field and finish by the other. Hence, each soul receives a particular destiny that may be long or short, more or less arduous, for the fulfillment of which it receives from nature, upon the order of God, the necessary faculties and forces.

Thus, everything beneficent or useful within us is only a loan, and our sole merit consists in making it fructify. Everything harmful or malevolent within us is a reactive agent, and our demerit is not the recognition of our evil, but giving to seductive evil our consent.

Hence, the souls whom the Father destines to lead some flock, he endows with more active virtues: physical, social, animic, intellectual, spiritual; but for these chosen souls, this preferential treatment is their most formidable test, because it implies a longer journey, more experiences, and the constant temptation to believe in their strength, their intelligence, their importance—to believe in themselves, to be full of themselves. But when creatures become full of themselves, the uncreated no longer descends into them: it finds no place there.

Hence, the Father cannot anymore employ this creature—this person congested with self-pride—for the office for which he had fitted him out. He then forsakes him, abandoning him to the fatality he has fashioned with his own hands—to the pitiless gods, to the agents of retaliation—until such time as he recognizes his fault and becomes humble. But in the interim, God gives this function of faithful servant to some other soul, to some poor, denuded one, in whom he replaces what natural faculty and virtues are absent by a gift of his supernatural grace.

This is what happens, generally speaking. But there are exceptions. Since the time of Jesus, there is one people that has not failed the divine mandate; there are a few disciples, at least one per century, who have fulfilled their role. Nevertheless; such disciples and such countries are unknown, and must remain unknown.

You can see how Israel, for example, originally chosen to

Reception of Grace

become the universal spokesman of the Redeemer, was stripped of this privilege by its callousness; while populations that were pagan, but humble and repentant as well, were the propagators of Christianity. And so it happens that our Lord exalts the humble and overthrows the mighty, placing the former to the fore and the latter to the rear. That is why he hides his secrets from scholars and reveals them to the ignorant. This is also how the Pharisees and the Doctors keep rejecting the designs of God that concern them.

As far as our inner, personal life is concerned, you know very well how insignificant we are, and that, in spite of our nothingness, we must give our all to our professions, our books, our fields of endeavor, to our machines, and to all those who have need of us.

But, if you have reached this wonderful equilibrium between invincible energy and peaceful detachment, remember: the crowd to which we belong is still a long way yet from such harmony. The white race, until now, has particularly known the ardor of discoveries, of conquests, and of initiative. It has penetrated everywhere. It has enslaved everything: foreign people, unknown forces, the secrets of matter, and the arcana of thought. But the white race has forgotten this promise of Christ: "Seek ye first the kingdom of God and all things will be added unto you." Had our race sought nothing else, it would have received mastery over forces, knowledge of secrets, and comprehension of the mysteries that remain totally closed to it even today.

The enemy of Christ has been well aware of this error, and for the past century has aggravated it. He has mobilized the soul of Asia, which as we know is adorned with prestigious attractions, bathed in perfumes, and clothed with the splendors of artifice—all much more fascinating than the nudity of its ideologies. The Slavic, German, and Anglo-Saxon races let themselves be drawn into the spell of these alluring charms—crowned with the seeming halo of sweetness, tolerance, and serenity. The critical and traditionalist spirit of the Latins at least immunizes them somewhat. But vigilant we must be. This famous "Yellow Peril" that our statesmen somewhat ridicule might come from the whole of Asia, and will probably overtake us through esthetics, philosophy, and psychology before drowning us in the blood of gigantic battles. Let us keep our hearts tightly entwined to the maxims of Christ.

Our Contemporaries

EVERY OBSERVER has the right of choosing his own point of view. As for us, we always try to look at things from the point of view of eternity. It is a better observatory than the one on Sirius that Renan chose. Sirius is of course very distant; but, being situated in the same space as we are, its distance reduces things and makes everything here-below seem insignificant. In this way, everything loses its importance, and the Renanian observer quickly arrives at scepticism. The point of view of eternity, being on the contrary situated at an incommensurable and infinite distance, finds itself close to all corners of finite space: it diminishes nothing; it keeps for each phenomenon its exact importance; it permits an exact appreciation of everything.

The ironic celebrity would exclaim: "Doubtless! But what do you do to reach God's point of view? Do you possess a mysterious recipe, are you superhuman beings, or do you merely adjust your faith to your imagination?"

Reception of Grace

The problem, as you know, is not as difficult as the rationalists think it to be. To solve it, one need only believe in the gospel, to the letter, and grant to it a total, plenary, and universal significance. And so, regarding the subject that I offer to your consideration today, the majority of our contemporaries seem at first sight to be divided; on the other side, there is the overwhelming majority who do not believe in Jesus as the only Son of God, as God himself; then again, alongside the others, there is a tiny minority of those who believe in this incomprehensible divinity. So, on the one hand is a loud, vociferous crowd taking great pains but attaining only fleeting results; on the other hand is a small and silent minority who think of nothing but Christ, who work for Christ alone, and whose every act exudes love for him.

The truth in the viewpoint of these latter is proven through the quality of their works. On the other hand, the others, no matter how flagrant their success may seem to be, quickly slip into oblivion, sink into the mud, and are splashed with the blood of their victims—their gyrations engendering nothing more than bitter recriminations and more agitation.

When Jesus compares his contemporaries to unruly children who create havoc in the streets and become vexed when they do not attract the attention of their elders, he is therewith sketching the portrait of our present generation as well. The twentieth century bears an astounding resemblance to the first century. We have: a large political and Caesarian civilization; citizens whose only concern is to twist the laws around; heads of state who are either cynics or utopians; a morbid taste for what is artificial, excessive, and unknown; a self-satisfied incomprehension of God;

THE HEALINGS OF CHRIST

frightful wars and catastrophes. But then again, here and there are a few small, unknown islands of light, upon which, unseen by the public, descends the ray of supernatural certitude.

Between such chronological periods there exist correspondences that certain researchers have brought to our attention. For instance: in the realm of philosophy, Charles Barlet brought it out in his *Essai sur l'évolution de l'Idée*; in the realm of history, Major Bruck brought it out in his works. And the Chinese sages believe that the pattern of evolution is a spiral wound around a cone, the base and apex of which are beyond our means of investigation; if we choose any of the generatrixes of this cone, the points where it intersects the spiral bear some resemblance to each other.

Yes, cosmic life is a perpetual beginning-again, but with elevations of level; knowledge of the past therefore serves to guide us in the present; and the older the individual, the longer the social body lasts, the wiser each should become. Both are undoubtedly improving—not as much as they should have, but less than they could if they did not let themselves be seduced indefinitely by "the games and songs and dances," as Jesus says. It is because of this dissipation and dispersion that the understanding of divine things develops so slowly. Today, just as twenty centuries ago, when a man repents, and through voluntary restitutions or voluntary privations tries to attenuate the evil he has committed, the public says he is crazy, that religion is gloomy and fanatical, that one should not follow a hard and vindictive God. Today, just as twenty centuries ago, when a man filled with the spirit proclaims a loving and compassionate God, lives in the peace of innocence, and spreads miracles of forgiveness and salvation around him, these same people

Reception of Grace

proclaim that man a hypocrite who takes life easy under the cover of religion.

These calumnies and slanders should not move the sincere disciple. If fraternal love inspires him, far from openly blaming his contemporaries, he will even forbid himself to judge them in his own conscience, so as not to render them responsible for the scandal their criticisms might provoke; and also, so as not to feed the discord they have created. This disciple's thoughts are: "People are what they can be, and understand only what they can understand; my mission is not to rectify their trespasses, but to come to their aid when they need it. Were they to attack my body, I would have to defend it insofar as it serves me, but without my becoming the attacker. When they attack me morally, however, they attack the self—and that I do not have to defend. Better for evil to be aimed at me than at one of my brothers. Also, if they believe me to be fanatical, might it not be my indiscreet zeal that shocks them? If they believe me as well to be easy-living, am I certain I have never taken advantage of the comforts heaven brings me, of the favors heaven grants me?"

Having given himself totally to God, the disciple considers all that happens to be good. For him, everything becomes a joy, becomes a reason for shedding pride and giving thanks. Circumstances are then such that, from this moment on, we disciples must deem ourselves very grateful for having received the strength to take our first steps upon that path—which is the path to peace. Let us then become very small within and rest in his peace.

Consider the Precursor: his life of penitence scandalized people. Consider Jesus: his normal and simple life scandalized people as well. They were both entirely right; it was their critics who were wrong. But these contradictory scandals generated, by reaction, more solid enthusiasms.

We, who have no public mission, we do not have to provoke any such salutary scandals. One of the causes that may provoke our lack of self-confidence, our inner turmoils, our dissatisfactions, are due to the insignificant scandals we sometimes incite in spite of ourselves in the small circle of our visible or invisible environment. We are still too "outward," too important, too much of this world, in our spiritual life.

We are well aware that we must observe the exigencies and duties of our outer life, made up of our family, profession, and social life; and that these obligations must be executed thoroughly and to the very best of our ability. We naturally will seek to acclimatize ourselves to live all these functions according to the spirit in which they must be lived. So kindly forgive me if I keep on repeating that you must do nothing unless it is done for Christ, in order to help him, to obey him, so that he will feel that you do love him a little.

Then, except for those for whom you are responsible—your children, servants, employees—remember that your example remains the best of sermons. Doubtless, a cordial reminder does some good; but the minute we moralize, the person to whom it is addressed feels we place ourselves above him and that we judge him. Unfortunate reactions follow, and debts are contracted by the critic.

Finally, and this sums it all up, be small; if you don't manage on your own to put pride under your feet, then get pushed around, get trampled underfoot by others. Consider how perfectly we are nothing; how nothing that is ourselves is ours; how nothing that we do is meritorious.

Reception of Grace

Yes, make yourselves very small within yourselves. Deprive your self of its earthly nourishment, make it fast, give it to eat what it does not like; force it to hard work.

But let no one see you undergoing such rigorous disciplines. As soon as one of these efforts becomes so difficult that people may read its traces on your face, run and lock yourself in. And there, where no one can see you, work and reason with that self; pray and meditate until such time as the feeling of certitude and of peace returns to restore serenity to your heart.

The Kingdom of God, Space, and Time

UNTIL NOW, we generally attributed to space and time a uniform mode to which all distances and durations conformed. For instance, classical astronomy measures planetary distances and their periods with the same yardstick used in land-surveying, and with the same cycles used in chronology.

Some thinkers have asked whether things happen on other planets similarly to what happens on earth. On close observation, certain mechanical, electrical, magnetic, even psychopathic, phenomena seem to indicate that space and time develop in reciprocal dependence, and that they can manifest themselves under other modes "within" those that the self registers. These findings, daring as they may seem, agree with ancient theories of esotericism, which affirmed and tended to prove that there are worlds of more than, or of less than, three dimensions, and durations of time where the past, the present, and the future are classified differently—in quantity and in quality—from the usual order.

THE HEALINGS OF CHRIST

This is all quite exact, just as it is true in mechanics that the mass of bodies and their energy are identical; that all natural forces are substances, are matter that has actual weight; that any ponderable matter is a force for the denser form, and matter for the subtler form. In physics, theories have just begun to be modified radically; they will be modified still more in the next fifty years. But just as within the positive science of the laboratory there is the equally positive science of esotericism, so within the latter, and beyond it, lies mystical science which, similarly to the other two, is experimental. There is no science without experimentation.

Other men, far rarer than the thinkers and adepts, have returned, in regard to space and time, as in many other matters, to the formula of common opinion: there is only one space and one time—qualifying further, however: "in the kingdom of God"; and that everywhere else, each universe has its own mode of extension and duration. These men know that a state of being can be experienced where everything is present and actual, where the millennial past coincides under the seer's glance with the indecipherable future, just as Paris and Peking, Thebes and the future cities of Australia, coincide under his gaze. This state is called "eternal life," and by a miracle that has been inexplicable to reason since Jesus, all those who want to accede to this impossible state can do so if they absolutely set their will to that end.

This absolute will consists in the crucifixion of all that is the self, by means of the love-sacrifice: the self, built up from selfishness, atavisms, and the residues of personalist analyses and experiences, wears out its strength resisting the resurgence of the non-self; it goes, and can only go, towards the multiple. Sacrifice, on the contrary, leads towards the unity

Reception of Grace

of eternal life, because this is nothing other than the permanent, the continuous, the identical, from which epochs, places, and creatures emerge. Christ's salvation enables us to live in the uncreated, even on this earth. Because of this, his salvation is the only real one; the salvations offered by other saviors are but halting-places, provisional solutions, unstable resolutions of human instability.

The kind of will the mystical effort demands does not recognize any limits to its development. It exerts itself and stretches to the realms beyond the possible. It denies what is absurd, risks everything for the whole, and, from each of these excesses of tension, is reborn and renewed afresh. Just as an athlete's thorax develops during his training, and the bones and muscles grow cell upon cell, so the will of the disciple to whom the seed was given, or in whom it is inborn, develops through each of the small energies liberated from the self by means of each small sacrifice. This growth is concrete; our whole person contributes to it: the fibers of our muscles just as much as the globules in our blood, the wave-lengths of our magnetism as much as the imponderable sparks of our mental faculties. In its basic root, the will is *faith*. Some people are born with faith in money, some have faith in art, others have faith in God. Our sole merit, our usefulness, is to put this spiritual seed to work, more or less patiently and courageously. The more sublime is our ideal, the greater the risks. The one who tries to conquer the divine must beware of considering the objects of his faith as subjective creations of his idealistic desires. Yes, God and eternal life are within us, but they are also, and primarily, outside us. They are not us: they took upon themselves to descend into us; and in order for us to reascend to their own place, they want the full collabora-

THE HEALINGS OF CHRIST

tion of our free-will—that spark of the Uncreated without which we would not be human beings anymore but merely thinking animals.

The mystic soars over the intelligible universe just as the philosopher hovers over the sensate universe. To him, faith proves everything; to him, faith makes everything real. Faith summons every thing and every creature before him. his earthly existence receives and becomes the very life of his eternity because he makes it become a continuous testimony of the veracity of eternal words. His entire being, intelligence, body, and soul have grasped and incorporated them all here on earth; in return, they take hold of him and realize him above. Hence, this man lives upon a special world, one created by the incarnation of the Word, a world equilibrated between the finite and the infinite, between time and eternity.

It might appear that these explanations do not explain anything, because the spiritual feat of which I am speaking belongs to the domain of being rather than to the domain of knowledge—and because theory, as opposed to practice, does not give complete knowledge. For instance, a writer does not only read literary masterpieces, he undertakes to write. The mystic, who is primarily a person of the will, becomes a man of action by necessity. Life interests him more than knowledge, although emotion and thought are always interwoven. Perhaps the following considerations will prove more telling.

Science has discovered facts that now lend to the most fantastic dreams of poets or seers an unexpected verisimilitude. Today, one knows that light, magnetism, and electricity possess weight; that time is a relative measure; that bodies when in motion change form (are deformed); that

Reception of Grace

perfect immobility does not exist, any more than does perpetual motion; that everything is alive, even so-called inorganic bodies; that the most inert bodies, even a crystal or a rail of iron, offer in the modifications of their internal structure phenomena that seem to be the first steps of biological acts such as the reparation of a wound, or of mental acts such as memory. Here we come back to the great antediluvian symbolism of Cain (the centripetal force of devouring time) and Abel (the centrifugal force of unendingly murdered space). We begin to understand, philosophically speaking, that there is an intelligible, abstract space and time, and then a concrete, measurable space and time relative to our faculty of perception; psycho-physiology has in fact demonstrated that the smallest duration our psyche can become aware is equal to two thousandths of a second, and the smallest measurable interval of space is a few thousandths of a millimeter.

Physics and chemistry, invading the domain of psychology in this way, lead us to follow the trail of Leibniz and Spinoza to the negation of free will. When we make a decision, men of science say we do it for conscious motives, motives of which we are aware; moreover, they say, our conscious being is a determined whole irrevocably fixed by destiny (fatality), itself the result of our education, surroundings, habits, and schooling. Furthermore, they say, we also make decisions owing to an incursion from the unconscious, itself the product of our overall heredity combined with the innumerable unknown heredities of all the energies converging from all points of the universe to construct our personality. We would therefore be, according to this account, a combination of latent forces, always ready to be exteriorized, and actual forces, triggered by the former

THE HEALINGS OF CHRIST

and by external reactions. Such, indeed, is, the psychological position of natural man.

The same thinkers state that a normal, just, and true act results from an exact knowledge of the realities of the milieu wherein it is to be accomplished. In his book *La Philososphie moderne*, Abel Rey writes, "You only act properly if you really know what you are doing." This, however, is the opposite of what Boutroux and Bergson teach. The tricky part is to obtain this exact knowledge of external and internal realities. Bergson is wrong, if I may say so, to do away with judgment, to advise only obedience to the vital instinct (*élan vital*). Boutroux is also wrong, in advising the use of reason, to call reason an intuitive, i.e., imprecise, feeling of truth. William James and the pragmatists are wrong to claim that the criterion of an act is the utility of its practical results. These three schools are wrong not only from a positivist point of view, but also from a mystical one. The criterion of the true act is its altruism (always opposite to the vital instinct), the clarity of its motives, its goodness rather than its utility.

But if, within me, ideas of obedience to God, charity, renunciation, and sacrifice (it matters not which) arise, whether as a fortuitous play of my unconscious, a consequence of my education, a mystical enlightenment; if, by analyzing my motives right down to the roots of my temperament, my character, and my mentality, I take the opposite decision to those to which these fateful elements would push me, would I not be approaching the state of freedom?

Of course my act will not be totally free, since my knowledge will not be complete, nor my will all-powerful; but I will have taken a step towards something new, towards the unexperienced, towards liberation. I will have grubbed

Reception of Grace

energies out of the soil of determinism. I will have begun to transport them to the land of liberty. This will seem that much the more plausible when, having agreed with all physicists that time, space, mass, and energy are inseparable and interdependent, I decide to go in the direction opposite from the one towards which my heredity, milieu, inertia, or energy were pushing me.

Anyhow, this mystical theory, or rather this élan of our effective power, would not have such great power were it non-existent. In the rational or scientific order there cannot be any contingencies, any miracle, free will, or divinity. But in the affective order, in the mystical or metaphysical realm, there is God, there are miracles, and there is freedom. Positivism will state: these are illusions. But no! Man cannot feel or experience inexistent things. The heart and the brain collaborate—never will they be lost one in the other. Let us not repeat the errors in logic made by Victor Cousin.

Let us imagine a man who, on every occasion, would decide against his innate or acquired tendencies; a man in whom the affective power, leading to the volitional power and the realizing power, would be strong enough to act always towards altruism, sacrifice, and renunciation. Such a man, a perfect disciple of Christ, will not deserve the reproaches that scholars rightly level at artists and metaphysicians. He will be a lucid and judicious mind, for isn't the ideal of the scientific spirit complete independence and rigorous impartiality? He will have a clear and straightforward will, for aren't people reputed to be energetic usually slaves to passion? He will have an enthusiastic heart, for nothing sublime can be attempted without enthusiasm. Doesn't such a man, able to dominate himself in the tumult of emotional storms, able to act despite all the poisons of fail-

THE HEALINGS OF CHRIST

ure, fatigue, and melancholy, break his spiritual chains? Certainly. He will wear them out, link by link, one after the other, from the most external, the most fragile, to the most secret, the most solid. Little by little he will extend his domination all the way to the unconscious, since his actions will contain an ever-greater share of free will.

What does Christ say? "Seek ye the truth and the truth shall make you free." It is a fact that man by himself cannot become free. He may reach the enclosure walls of his prison, but someone else must open the door for him—the Holy Spirit. And the ceremony of this opening? You know it. We spoke of it some time ago: it is the baptism of the Spirit, over which our Christ-the-Word presides.

People will say this is quite a venturesome theory, and rather naive. Venturesome? No, if we refer to the unanimous tradition of the followers of Christ. No again, if we accept the conclusions of a philosophy based on science. In fact, in the universe, this philosophy does not merely show us water-tight partitions between what is true and what is false, between accuracy and inexactness, between the visible and the invisible, the continuous and the discontinuous, the full and the empty, the organic and the inorganic, matter and force, body and soul, evil and good; rather, between the once separate terms of these binaries, this philosophy shows us, I say, a series of numerous and delicate gradations: it is on the march towards discovery of the unity of life. One day we will realize that space and time are not abstractions, but substantial environments, such as energy, light, and magnetic fields. We have already recognized the properties hitherto exclusive to matter: inertia, weight, and structure. We will then possess a "gospel" view of things; we will know that all things live an organic life with different degrees of intelligence. Instead of detecting nothing but determinism everywhere, we will find nothing but freedom everywhere. We will understand the saying of St John that each and every form and being embraces a "life," a "truth," and a "way."

The episodes where Jesus hears, sees, and acts from a distance, and where the miraculous effect occurs at the very moment of his action, can be explained by the facts whose mechanism I am trying to indicate. The worlds are only the inverted shadows of eternal objects. How could a thing that can be measured by our senses or our logic be divine? The kingdom of God penetrates the universe and ourselves to the very depths. All that is necessary is to accept this blessed invasion; it is a matter question settling into the irrational. Constructing, as the apologists do, a set of hypotheses that lead to mystical concepts is not faith. Faith does not look for proofs; faith is simple, unassuming, total. God's words seem so real to faith that the idea of an obstacle or delay to their fulfillment doesn't even cross its mind. But for God to deign to come down and dwell within us, we must first have learned to cling to nothing for ourselves.

And these miracles where Jesus commands time and distance are words of unity, of absoluteness, and eternity that we have to live, to incorporate into our perishable selves, to embody at last.

The Son of the Centurion

ONE DAY, on his return north to Galilee, Jesus, from a distance, healed the son of an officer of Capernaum. This city may be taken to represent the earth; the officer, the self; his dying son, the intellect. What about Jesus? He is Jesus.

THE HEALINGS OF CHRIST

Here on earth, woefully, our intelligence often grows faint and our heart often has need of a reaction from the outside, of a miracle, in order to become sensitive to the light again. But to believe only after having received proof of divine power is not faith. Faith is believing and being convinced without proof, on just a simple word from God. As soon as there is any kind of approximative reasoning, faith is lacking. Faced with a miracle, a sceptic argues, invokes the play of coincidences, of poorly conducted statistics, and scientific explanations; but those who witness that same miracle, those in whom the light has not quite been buried under ashes, will feel the intuitive flash through which the experiences of the spiritual man manifest themselves to the physical man.

When you are facing an insoluble difficulty, or at the due date of bills without a cent to pay them, or when illness has drawn you to the brink of death, you know that the test is warranted, and that having acted wrongly in the past, ruin or death would be justice. Yet, if you have faith, my example is not meant for you, because only the truly liberated man (the new man) possesses faith—and neither worry, anguish, nor suffering have any claim upon him, save when he shoulders them to relieve others. If you do not have faith, you can either let yourself go, or fight with all of your intelligence and energy, or cry out for help to anyone in the visible or invisible world. Heaven abandons the inert; heaven helps the proud who believe in themselves just enough to give them a chance to put their strength to work. But you who are a disciple, you know that heaven sees and watches over you, and that in spite of your being lukewarm, heaven will never let you perish.

Consequently, you remain calm; you even see to it that

Reception of Grace

close acquaintances or friends cannot read anguish on your face. You seem as gay and as lively as usual and... you wait to lock yourself in your closet to cry. Then you speak to Christ and say: "Lord, I have deserved these misfortunes and many others; I am not worthy to have you cast your gaze upon me; but you can heal me, save me from ruin, console my despair. I submit to your decision. Save me if you think it right. I promise I will try, with your help, to do better." These are beautiful words, the sentiment is noble, and the saints act accordingly. But even so, it is not faith. It is only the path by means of which one reaches it.

Were we able to define, comprehend, or even imagine faith, it would cease to belong to the supernatural. Let us make the necessary effort that enables us to receive it as a gift. Let us always go to the end of our strength, to the limit of our endurance and of our courage. This offering of the possible irresistibly evokes the impossible.

Let us train ourselves to express our faith. An increasing number of our brothers will have need of us to call upon the angels of faith, and so will our country. Let us remain worthy of the circumstances.

⊕

Healing from a distance can be effectuated in different ways. If the operator is an ordinary man whose psychic powers are in the process of being developed, but who does not follow the path of the gospel, this man will act either by means of magnetism, by means of the invisibles, or by the will.

When using the magnetic process, the operator makes passes as if the patient were in the room, or by having a medium go in search of the double of the patient, or by

THE HEALINGS OF CHRIST

having the medium carry the fluid to the patient, or by having the patient drink a magnetized potion, or by having him wear a magnetized object, or by magnetizing some of the clothing or an object impregnated by the effluvia of the patient. There also exist processes to extricate and manipulate such fluids contained in running water, in stones, and in plants.

Acting through the invisibles consists either of calling upon spirits, a transference, a magical evocation or conjuration, or an invocation to the auxiliaries attached to each religious community in the prescribed form.

Acting through thought consists of constructing a mental image of healing and projecting it onto the patient. Or you can argue, as the Christian Scientists do, but from a distance.

Acting through will is done by suggestion, verbal or mental; or by commanding the disease to leave.

None of these methods are lawful in themselves; some are sheer misuse of power, the others are sheer imprudence. In short, nothing is lawful when it does not have recourse to God. The only one who can practice a healthy and direct therapy without spiritual risks is the one who will conform to the doctrines of the gospel, who will acknowledge that life, intelligence, and free-will is owed each creature, who who will practice universal charity and expects nothing, save through prayer. That one may make use of magnetism, since it is a normal power, just as muscular force, nervous energies, and cerebral faculties are normal powers—but he will use it in all humility, concurrently with prayer. He will abstain from all mediumistic processes, because no one knows whom one calls. He will abstain from using magic and mental or willful processes because they are constraints,

Reception of Grace

and no creature has the right of tyranny over another. So, should prayer be the only recourse for the disciple who tries to heal? Certainly, yes. But there are cases where healing would be inopportune, in which case simple human magnetism can be employed.

The advanced disciple, the "soldier" of Christ, has at his command a more subtle, unknown, and more powerful magnetism that has been brought on earth by Christ, and that only those who perfectly practice the precepts of charity are endowed with. Ordinary magnetism obeys certain laws, those of polarity, places, days, and hours; it acts with greater or lesser power according to the physiological state or to the training of the operator. Mystical magnetism is free—neither time, distance, circumstance, nor anything physical checks it. No matter what the age, health, or state of the milieu where healer or patient may find themselves, it accomplishes its mission, its action, because it comes in a direct line from the works of Christ. Do not try to attain it through your own means; it would escape you. Execute the law of Christ to its very fundament, as best you can, and pray. That is all. Any other attempt is useless.

Moreover, all I have said only serves as an introduction and habituation to the state of being that will be ours when we will have received the faculty of acting in the Kingdom as well as on earth simultaneously, and with full awareness. Then we will live upon the plane of One, of Unity.

Regarding the Supernatural

CHRIST IS THE ONLY one among the founders of religions who has dared to ask his followers to sacrifice their self for the sake of charity, to harbor superhuman optimism on

THE HEALINGS OF CHRIST

account of hope, to negate or rather surpass all intellectual concepts, and to overthrow all so-called impossibilities by virtue of faith. Other religions rely on metaphysics, such as Taoism; on philosophy, such as Buddhism; on experimental data of secret sciences, such as Brahmanism or Mazdeism; on a voluntary and dogmatic affirmation, such as Mosaism and Islamism; or, finally, on a feeling of community with all other creatures, such certain contemplative sects subsidiary to the mother religions.

Christ alone places man face to face with God without intermediaries other than himself, who is one with God. He alone reveals the formal secret of creation within us, showing creation to be but the shadow, limited by space and time, of the eternal, infinite, limitless kingdom that he inhabits. He alone makes us aware that all created values are inverse to the non-created. Finally, he alone proposes to mankind—seduced as we are by the cold lights of abstractions, yet specially avid to comprehend—how to probe the depths of living knowledge by the soul's soaring towards supernatural realities, and by the most inflexible and strictest discipline of the self.

The gospel alone obliges us to be as self-exacting, vigilant, critical of our faults, lucid, and impartial as the true scientist who tests and analyzes the secrets of matter in his laboratory; and at the same time it encourages us to nourish a sensitivity as rich, an enthusiasm as lyrical, as those of the artist and the poet. The gospel aims to make us balanced and complete beings.

The true mystic is healthy. If during the ordinary course of his life a seer or psychic does not demonstrate thoughtful appreciation, good sense, and realism, one may conclude that his visions are false. When the ecstasy is true, it does

Reception of Grace

not debilitate the mental faculties; on the contrary, it strengthens them. For instance, study the lives of true ecstatics in detail, among them St Vincent de Paul, St Bernard, St Colette, St Theresa, Madame Acariem, and the Cure d'Ars (to name but a few), and you will find that these servants of God (whom some superficial critics deem to be neurotics) were masters in the art of solving difficult situations, whether in psychological or financial matters, or in the various social, family, or political questions. But, whether they were fervently pious, consumed by their desire for heaven, or possessed of a delicate sensitivity, they nevertheless exercised upon themselves—upon their character, temperament, intellect, likes and dislikes—a most autocratic government.

To understand Christ, one must not study him as Renan, Ledrain, Loisy, or Alfred Charbonnel have done. It is also useless to explain him according to Taine, or as Fr Didon did. Why? Because Jesus is not a personage belonging to history alone; because his formation was not influenced by either his race or his milieu; because his parables were not allegories; and, finally, because it is sacrilegious to undertake, as the Dominican Father Didon did, to give the words of Jesus "more spark to set them off."

One must visualize the Son of God such as he is: the untiring voyager scouring the worlds, laden with all the sorrows, and shouldering all the ordeals and tests too heavy for our pride to bear; exhausted by sacrifices and night vigils; impelled by his great, compassionate love—yet drawing from the well of his agonies the strength of resurrecting ceaselessly for his additional martyrdoms.

The seeming folly of establishing Christianity (given the minimal means available to it in its first beginnings) proves its Founder to have been superhuman. If, in spite of the errors and faults of its workmen, this doctrine still subsists after twenty centuries, it is because it contains and possesses something divine. The task of the Christian is to maintain this imperishable light aglow, to free it from dense, obscure, earthly smokes and ashes. This task is called: the conquest of sanctity.

God has organized all creation with the sole object of leading us to sanctity. God pursues us everywhere. The criminal, the pervert, the shallow man, the laggard—we are all his prey. He lies in wait for us, hounds us from thicket to thicket, until at last, worn and disgusted from the vain delights of the world, we succumb to the mighty thunderbolts of his love. We are the beloved children of the Father. We are the unique concern of the Son. We are the fortunate victims of the Holy Spirit.

But to see truth, we must cross the threshold closed the glamorous veils of appearances. Let us analyze our certitudes and our doubts down to the axiom necessarily found at the origin of each of these. Then, if we take the opposite axiom, we can deduce, by logical sequence, certainties and doubts contrary to the starting-points of our first inductions. From these antitheses, we usually conclude that everything is plausible and possible, and that everything is therefore uncertain. In order to enter into the mystical phalanx, one must then find a third point of departure, a third set of axioms that reunites and conciliates the preceding theses. This is how one enters intellectually into gospel poverty. You already know the way one enters into it morally. From that time on, one begins to say: I know nothing; and: I can do nothing. Into this double emptiness surges plenitude; into this doubly dark night explodes the ray; prayer

Reception of Grace

begins with murmurs; one starts walking on the path; truth appears and life descends; the temporal horizons fade into the shadows, while the immemorial landscapes of faith rise before our expectant and wonder-struck eyes.

This is the school one has to follow in order to accept the Incarnation of the Word, in order to understand the miracles of Jesus Christ, to permit the approach of the Spirit, through whom it will be possible for us, at a later date, to copy our model. When speaking to you of the healings of Jesus in such details, I have wanted nothing but to make the mystical universe more accessible to you. Whoever has caught a glimpse of the splendor of this kingdom of glory carries forever in his bosom the salvational nostalgia; and this immortal torment will someday prostrate him before the tree of the cross, whose fruits are peace, happiness, omniscience, omnipotence, and liberty.

CHAPTER IV

The Kingdom of Heaven

NE OF THE PHARISEES invited Jesus to a meal; so he went into the Pharisee's house and took his place at the table. And there was then a sinful woman in the city, who, hearing that he was at the table in the Pharisee's house, brought a pot of ointment with her, and took her place behind him at his feet, weeping; then she began washing his feet with her tears, and drying them with her hair, kissing his feet, and anointing them with the ointment. His host, the Pharisee, saw it, and thought to himself, "If this man were a prophet, he would know who this woman is that is touching him, and what kind of woman, a sinner." But Jesus, addressing him said, "Simon, I have a word for thy hearing." "Tell me, Master." He answered: "There was a creditor who had two debtors; one owed him five hundred pieces of silver, the other fifty; they had no means of paying him, and he gave them both their discharge. And now tell me, which of them loves him the more?" "I suppose," Simon answered, "that it is the one who had the greater debt discharged." Jesus said, "Thou hast judged rightly." Then he turned towards the woman, and said to Simon, "Dost thou see this woman? I came into thy house, and thou gavest me no water for my feet; yet she has washed my feet with her tears, and wiped them with her hair. Thou gavest me no kiss of greeting; she has never ceased to kiss my feet since I entered. Thou didst not pour oil on my head; yet she has anointed my feet, and with ointment. And so, I tell thee, if great sins have been forgiven her, it is

THE HEALINGS OF CHRIST

because she has greatly loved. He loves little, who has little forgiven him." Then he said to the woman, "Thy sins are forgiven." And his fellow guests thereupon thought to themselves, "Who is he, that he even forgives sins?" But he told the woman, "Thy faith has saved thee; go in peace."

Then followed a time in which he went on journeying from one city or village to another, preaching and spreading the good news of God's kingdom. With them were the twelve apostles, and certain women whom he had freed from evil spirits and from sicknesses: Mary who is called Magdalene (from Magdala in Galilee), who had had seven devils cast out of her, and Joanna, the wife of Chusa, Herod's steward, and Susanna, and many others, who ministered to him with the means they had.

As he began to teach by the seaside again, a great multitude gathered before him, so that he went and sat in a boat while all the multitude was on the land, at the sea's edge. He taught them in parables. "Here is a sower gone out to sow. And as he sowed, there were some grains that fell beside the path, so that they were trodden underfoot and the birds flew down and ate them. And others fell on rocky ground, where the soil was shallow; these sprang up all at once, because they had not sunk deep in the ground, and when the sun rose they were parched; they had taken no root, and so they

The Kingdom of Heaven

withered away. Some fell among brambles, so that the brambles grew up with them and smothered them. Others fell where the soil was good, and these sprouted and grew, and yielded a harvest: some of them thirtyfold, some sixtyfold, some a hundredfold." "Listen," he exclaimed, "you that have ears to hear with, hear!"

When they could speak with him alone, his disciples who were with him asked why he spoke in parables. He answered them: "To you it is granted to penetrate the mysteries of God's kingdom; and if I talk to them in parables, it is because, though they have eyes, they cannot see, and though they have ears, they cannot hear or understand. Indeed, in them the prophecy of Isaiah is fulfilled:

'You will listen and listen, but for you there is no understanding;
You will watch and watch, but for you there is no perceiving;
For the heart of this people has become dull;
Their ears are slow to listen,
And they keep their eyes shut,
For fear their eyes might see,
For fear their ears might hear,
For fear their heart might understand,
For fear they might be converted,
For fear that I might heal them.'

"Listen to the sense of the parable of the sower: what the sower sows is the word of God. Those by the wayside who have the word sown in them are those who have listened, but no sooner have they heard it than Satan comes, and takes away this word that was sown in their hearts for fear they might be saved. In the same way, those who take in the seed in rocky ground are those who entertain the word with joy as soon as they hear it, and yet it does not take root in them; then faith lasts for a time, but afterwards, when tribulation or persecution arises over the word, their faith is soon shaken. And there are others who take in the seed in briars; they are those who hear the word but who allow the cares of this world and the deceitfulness of riches and their other appetites to smother the word so that it remains fruitless. Finally, there are those who take in the seed in good soil; they are those who hear the word and welcome it and yield a steady harvest, one grain thirtyfold, one sixtyfold, one a hundredfold."

And he said to them: "No one who lights a lamp brings it in to be put under a bushel measure, or under a bed, but places it on the lampstand so that those who come in may see it. What is hidden, is hidden only so that it may be revealed; what is kept secret, is kept secret only that it may come to light. Listen, all of you that have ears to hear with." And he said to them: "Look well what it is that you hear. The measure in which you give is the measure in which you will be repaid, and more will be given you besides. If a man is rich, gifts will be made to him; if he is poor, even the little he has will be taken away from him."

And again, he said: "What comparison shall I find for the kingdom of heaven? It is like leaven, that a woman has taken and buried away in three measures of meal, enough to leaven the whole batch. It is like a grain of mustard seed that a man has taken and planted in his garden, where it has thriven and grown

The Kingdom of Heaven

into a great tree, and all the birds have come and settled in its branches."

And he also said to them: "The kingdom of heaven is like this; it is as if a man should sow a crop in his land. Whether he goes to sleep and wakes again, night after night, day after day, the crop meanwhile sprouts and grows, without any knowledge of his. So, of its own accord, the ground yields increase: first the blade, then the ear, then the perfect grain in the ear. And when the fruit appears, then it is time for him to put in the sickle, because now the harvest is ripe."

All this Jesus said to the multitude in parables, and would say it in parables only that they might understand, and so fulfilling the words which were spoken by the prophet.

'I will speak my mind in parables;
I will give utterance to things which have been kept secret from the beginning of the world.'

Then, when alone with his disciples, he explained everything.

And again, he said: "What comparison shall I find for the kingdom of heaven? It is like leaven, that a woman has taken and buried away in three measures of meal, enough to leaven the whole batch."

And he put before them another parable: "The kingdom of heaven is similar to a man who sowed his field with clean seed; but while all his servants were asleep, an enemy of his came and scattered tares among the wheat, and was gone. So, when the blade had sprung up and come into ear, the tares, too, came to light; and the farmer's men went to him and said, 'Sir, was it not clean seed thou didst sow in thy field? How comes it, then, that there are tares in it?' He said, 'An enemy has done it.' And his men asked him: 'Wouldst thou then leave us go and gather them up?' He answered: 'No, because while you are gathering the tares you will root up the wheat with them. Leave them to grow side by side till harvest, and when harvest time comes I will give the word to the reapers: Gather the tares first, and tie them in bundles to be burned, and store the wheat in the barn.'"

Then he sent the multitude away, and went back into the house, where his disciples came to him, and said: "Explain to us the parables of the tares in the field." He answered: "It is the Son of Man that sows the good seed. The field is the world, and the sons of the kingdom are the good seed; the sons of the wicked one are the tares. The enemy that sowed them is the devil, and the end of the world is the harvest; the reapers are the angels. As the tares were gathered together and burned in the fire, so it will be when the world is brought to an end; the Son of Man will give charge to his angels, and they will gather up all those who give offense in his kingdom, all those who do wickedly in it, and will cast them into the furnace of fire, where there will be weeping, and gnashing of teeth. Then, at last, the just will shine out, clear as the sun, in their Father's kingdom. Listen, you that have ears to hear with.

"The kingdom of heaven is like a treasure hidden in a field; the man who finds it, hides it again, and now,

The Kingdom of Heaven

for the joy it gives him, is going home to sell all that he has to buy that field.

"Again, the kingdom of heaven is also similar to a trader looking for rare pearls, and when he finds one pearl of great cost, he sells all that he had and buys it.

"Again, the kingdom of heaven is like a net that was cast into the sea, which enclosed fish of every kind at once; when it was full, the fishermen drew it up, and sat down on the beach, where they stored all that was worth keeping in their buckets, and threw the useless kind away. So it will be when the world is brought to an end; the angels will go out and separate the wicked from the just, and will cast them into the furnace of fire, where there will be weeping, and gnashing of teeth.

"Have you grasped all this?" "Yes, Lord," they said to him.

And he said to them, "Every scholar, then, whose learning is of the kingdom of heaven must be like a rich man, who knows how to bring both new and old things out of his treasure-house."[1]

The Imitation of Jesus

IT IS SO TRUE that our activities are the step by step trek of our immortal spirit along the roads of the invisible, that the

---

[1] Luke 7:36–50; Luke 8:1–3; Matthew 13:10–15; Mark 4:10–13; Luke 8:4–15; Matthew 13:3–9, 18–23; Mark 4:3–9, 14–20; Luke 8:16–18; Mark 4:21–23; Matthew 5:15–16; Mark 4:24–25; Matthew 13:31–32; Mark 4:30–32; Luke 13:18–19; Mark 4:26–29; Matthew 13:34–35; Mark 4:33–34; Matthew 13:4, 13:33; Luke 13:20–21; Matthew 13:44–46.

THE HEALINGS OF CHRIST

fact of passing from a wide road to the narrow path is called a conversion. At certain times, when exhausted or jaded, we retrace our steps. And when this return is effected with the highest motives—or, if you prefer, is effected in our deepest psychological regions—the states of remorse, repentance, desolation, or intimate disaggregation that we undergo correspond to this backward march, to this "turning back," in the course of which we are obliged to make restitution to any of the victims of our selfishness those forces or substances we had taken from them unduly. This restitution is called penance.

Before the descent of the Word upon earth, men were obliged to pay their debts in full. This law was called karma by the Hindus, and the "law of retaliation" by Moses. And since, during the time it took sinners to acquit themselves of their debts, they were contracting new debts on account of new sins (for evil, once sown, develops, fructifies, and multiplies of itself), their payments were likewise indefinitely multiplying. Thus did human suffering also increase, perpetuating itself indefinitely. In short, man cannot save himself by himself. But the innocent and voluntary sufferings endured by the Word incarnate in Jesus Christ have the effect of placing at the disposal of the repentant sinner the inexhaustible succors of divine mercy, which theology calls grace because they are always "gratis." In fact, these mercies come from the Absolute; and because this is so, the least of them by its very nature is worth more than the merits of a creature from the Relative, no matter how colossal we imagine them to be.

Having understood this, let us begin to study the episode of the courtesan at the home of the Pharisee. There are many lessons to be found therein.

The Kingdom of Heaven

Jesus did not only visit the poor or people in modest circumstances; he also accepted invitations to the homes of the rich. He did not comport himself on grounds of utility or respectability. He flattered neither conservatives nor revolutionaries, since both are sometimes right and sometimes wrong. And just as he did not establish social paradises on economic or political reform alone, he did not choose his disciples, his familiars, or his occasional hosts on the basis of exterior considerations. For him, men, things, or circumstances were but pretexts to correct an error, to light a candle, to sow a seed. This world, which we labor in, which many believe to be the only one, was in his hands, only a reverse side. He acted on the other side of the weft, the right side, and it is because he saw what we do not see, that many of his gestures seem incomprehensible and many of his words unfathomable.

We may adopt a line of conduct parallel to his, though on a very much lower plane; but let us beware of the secret tendencies of our personality that may well sidetrack our most straightforward intentions. Each person is drawn to a particular social or worldly setting because of his tastes, his culture, his refinement, and his varied opinions. We excuse those who associate with the "scum" because they are not entirely responsible for the sordid quality of their sympathies, and it is only right to be indulgent. But then, he who has sensitivity, delicacy, and a refined type of mind does not gain much merit by associating with those of a like caliber. And the ones who like their comfort gain no merit by living among the rich. These three types merely follow their particular brand of selfishness. If, for instance, we choose to dine among elegant people, we must be frank enough to admit that it is because we like luxury and well-being, and

THE HEALINGS OF CHRIST

not because we are trying to emulate Jesus, who also sat at table with the opulent bourgeois of his time. And if, on the contrary, we like to slum around the back streets, let us not be hypocritical and claim that we do it because Jesus visited people of no consequence. Forgive me for making use of such commonplace examples, but we so readily delude ourselves, even lie to ourselves—and do so with such ingenious duplicity.

If, on the contrary, without heed to our own preferences, we go where we are called, particularly where we can soothe someone, ease a bitterness, open a window to hope, encourage someone to be resigned, appease a hatred, lessen prejudices, or just embellish a plain old home; in short, if we go where we would prefer not to go—*that* is imitating Jesus. Don't you realize that the sensitive delicacy of Jesus was tortured amid the inevitable ugliness of the oppressed? Don't you believe that the generous ardor of his soul overflowing with compassion was martyred by the stone-hearted selfishness of the so-called great who did not understand him, yet whose invitations he accepted? He was always to be found, here and there, whence even a single sigh addressed to the light was sounded. Listening but to that sigh, seeing nothing but the diverse distresses of both the unfortunate and the powerful, heedless of his own disgust, he heard nothing but sincere cries for help.

When reading the gospels, then, let us not so much grow attached to the charm of the stories or the marvels, as to the secret spirit that engenders some and animates others. It takes time for us to communicate with their delightful breath of eternal goodness. Great perseverance is needed for the perpetual effort of living its precepts. But each of our persevering efforts immediately receives its salary, indeed a

The Kingdom of Heaven

dual salary: desire to go forward, and ever-deeper comprehension of the universal Great Work.

And so, to resume, there is Jesus at the table of the Pharisee. It doesn't matter whether we represent the scene as accurately as our archeological knowledge allows, or whether we rely on the accounts of orientalists, novelists, visionaries, or simple travelers. These are artifices, undoubtedly legitimate, but external, to move our devotion.

Two or three writers have even imagined Christ as having returned, as living among us today, giving to our society the example and the teaching proper to our culture, our modern ideas and vices.

As for us, let us try to look at our model in a spiritual way. Beyond the visible aspects of his story, let us penetrate into the incommensurable radiance of his heart; let us climb towards the peaks of his spirit, where all mysteries lie; let us consider the sublime singularity of his person, the most unified, most coherent, one might imagine, and yet at the same time the most diverse and most subtle.

Here, visiting a well-known and reputable Pharisee, we find both God himself and the complete Man. He remains forever identical to self; and yet, without diminishment or alteration he is to be found in the very core of all that suffers and all that aspires for good: in the person of his host, in the persons of the guests, in the person of the woman who came in. Because suffering is to be found wherever he goes, the God-Man is at home wherever he goes. It is Jesus who satisfies the palate of the rich man whose heart has grown cold. It is Jesus who touches off despair in the wounded heart of the villain. It is Jesus who holds anger in check within the embittered heart of the criminal. All this he does, that our earthly disgust may give birth to a desire for heavenly goods; that our weariness may call forth young hope; that our impotent anger, brought to a climax, may become the first breaths of almighty gentleness.

Thus it is that fallen humanity marches on. Doubtless, faithful obedience to the gospels would grant us reprieve from these laborious reactions, yet rare are those who are capable of receiving light without having first lost themselves in the mire of darkness.

Hence, at the home of this Pharisee, we find the Word. Nobody recognizes him, however, for the mediocre souls of the host and of the guests, incapable of going far to the left, are equally unable to go far to the right. Mary Magdalene alone will see the truth. She had committed all excesses and has drunk their bitterness. Her ardent soul had rejected the grayish pride of despair. Hence, heaven had sent her repentance. She flung herself into repentance just as she had rushed headlong into the splendors of this world. She has sinned much and the Word has forgiven her much. Because she had received from him a superabundant pardon, she has loved him as no one ever loved him before.

God's love for us and our future love for him are really wholly unknown quantities. The indigence of our soul, the weakness of our mind, can neither be nourished nor move in the vertiginous world of spiritual love. The purest among us, when they have wanted to relate some of the echoes of unrevealed harmonies, have found it necessary to use the limited language of human love. To say of divine love that it is all sacrifice is really like announcing that the sun shines brightly. Eloquence becomes so banal, even to becoming common, when it attempts to describe the life of love; because this life of love differs as much from the life of the body and the life of our intellect as metaphysics differs from

The Kingdom of Heaven

science, or integral calculus differs from mathematics. Our affective powers, however sublime they may be, still need to relax, to regain their momentum, to overcome their weariness; they suffer setbacks all the more cruel for having offered themselves more candidly to ingratitude and incomprehension. Do we not see Jesus himself grow faint at the sight of the dark evils with which humankind responds to his loving tenderness? Every disciple also suffers his watch in the Garden of Gethsemane.

But when heaven on earth will have become a reality, fraternal love and divine love—having become brothers—will rise to an altitude that remains inconceivable today. The self-renewing love of each of the chosen ones, rejuvenated through each of its outpourings, unceasingly increased by the corresponding love of all the other chosen ones, will long know fatigue or worry. These souls, elevated beyond their own temporal limits, will blossom from infinity in a harmonious competition whose successive equilibriums, far from restricting their impulses, will forever exalt their ardor and spontaneity.

But that is the end; we are just at the beginning.

Mary Magdalene

HEAVEN IS WITH those who suffer most. While we are still on the road, it overlooks our faults, looking only at our distress. Its soldiers go wherever they have to go, but above all, like their Master, to the people who make the world go around, and who are given too little attention—they go with the people who are shunned, who frighten hypocrisy, who have perhaps fallen merely from want of proper care. That is why Jesus, in the home of the Pharisee, welcomes

THE HEALINGS OF CHRIST

the courtesan. What a scandal for the respectable man, the pillar of society! And for the woman, what admirable intuitive certainty of forgiveness!

One who strays far into evil is capable of going still further into righteousness. God's justice does not employ the same procedures as does human justice, which believes only in the law of retaliation—only in recent centuries has it acknowledged extenuating circumstances. Contrary to human logic, heaven pursues the stubborn one who seems the least worthy. The farther astray has that man wandered, the more he has become mired and fallen ill through his own fault, the more heaven watchfully awaits his first regret, his first call for help.

Such is divine love, and such must human love become. The character of divine love is self-sacrifice. Its modes of action are infinite. Its power knows no limit. Its essence is the ardent desire to serve the Beloved, even if it means losing him and losing oneself forever to obey him.

Love is capable of accepting and shouldering all chains, hence it is the freest of all beings. It knows neither time, distance, nor the impossible. It resists death. Love shines even in hell. Even mediocrity cannot tarnish it.

True love never frets; it shines forth in serenity, radiates in peace, immolates itself in beatitude. Misfortunes are but added fuel to feed its flame. Possessing immutable certitude, irresistible power, and sole truth, it hallows everything, because everything is an occasion for its growth.

It is because of her capacity to suffer that woman is closer to heaven than man. It is also the reason we should listen to her more than we do. But she should not have to step out of her role. She should not have to earn her daily bread outside of her home—for that is her place, and she is there to

The Kingdom of Heaven

embellish with idealism all the commonplaces of daily life, which are her concern. If she seriously wishes to accomplish her function, she has far more work than her husband. But her place is not in lecture halls, committees, in lists of protest and demands, and other illusory endeavors. Why should she concern herself with these feministic chimeras? If she is truly good, will she not feel in the very core of her heart that God is with the humble and the obscure workers?

All actions, even those that seem indifferent and pointless, have results; it is their motive that makes them more or less fruitful, according to its magnitude and sincerity. Note what this courtesan receives from having anointed her Master's feet.

On the one side we notice the respectable, wealthy, honorable, and well-meaning man: "a pillar of society." On the other is a woman outside the pale of the law, an object of scandal, a scorned flotsam of society. In the middle is the superhuman Being whose very presence judged each of them, unveiling the secrets of their spirit to their very depths. Here we have the so often misunderstood dual play of opposites that serves as pretext for the tyranny of the mighty and for the revolt of the weak. Most people bracket material power with spiritual grandeur. The crowd believes fortune, high positions, and mental superiority imply great moral qualities; those from higher social strata tend to look down upon the common man. Both are mistaken. They do not understand the inverse march between temporal power and spiritual knowledge. The downtrodden do not realize the corruptive force of gold and glory; those in authority shut their ears to the calls from the unfortunate. The great human antinomy is not that of intelligence versus ignorance; it is, rather, kindheartedness versus hardheartedness: the wealthy are not necessarily refined; the poor are not necessarily coarse. So our Pharisee, who occupies a high social position, is well-educated, conducts himself well, and expresses reasonable opinions, languishes further from God than does the scandalous woman who defies conventions and lives from day to day. This does not mean to imply that heaven prefers non-conformists to conventional people (after all, one meets many rich people whose sole concern is helping others, and poor people devoured by base passions), but that enjoyment of social privileges often withers the heart, while the gall and shame endured by those who follow the primrose path always results in awakening within them the spark of the Word, no matter how deeply hidden it is beneath the thick coating of ashes from shameful idolatries.

The Pharisee was a rationalist, the courtesan a budding mystic: the former lacked the notion of the limits of intelligence; the latter lacked the notion of discipline. Because he feels unduly proud of all his human prerogatives, the Pharisee does not feel God close to him, while the courtesan, in whom the explosion of repentance shatters and consumes, in the glow of this fire discovers before her her Lord and Savior.

This does not imply that we should disdain social advantages, natural gifts, or education, but that we should attribute to them only a relative and human value. This does not imply that we should gad about under the pretext of trying anything out merely for the sake of experience and of reaching wisdom through satiety, but that we must not stigmatize all those who are the unbalanced, all those who are disadvantaged, all those who are tossed about by the ebb

The Kingdom of Heaven

and flow of their appetites—for among this pitiful crowd there may be some whose very disequilibrium will bounce them back to God, whose disadvantaged lot will cast them onto the shores of grace, and whose self-disgust will give them a thirst for the eternal fountains.

Each one of us is also that city where Pharisees live in their beautiful, tidy houses, and courtesans in their luxurious mansions or in hovels. In us also the Master has passed through once; he sat down in one of our rooms that he had, from the beginning, adorned with the richest ornaments, that he had furnished with that reason, that logic, that memory, that realistic wisdom which gives us superior figures in the face of other beings. But these wonderful faculties, in their self-pride, did not recognize their Creator; while, in the less noble corners of our person, one of the tumultuous forces of instinct, hitherto greedy for the whole physical universe and solely occupied with conquering and revelling in it, sees up there an extraordinary glow, tastes an indescribable sweetness, hears an ineffable voice; it is what is most material and coarse in us that grasps the arch-subtle and the pure spirit.

The same holds true in the social order and in the ethnic order. Those peoples and races whom the Father elected from the very first to open the road of salvation for others, and endowed with all the needful gifts for this purpose, little by little came to consider these graces as belonging to them by right. Becoming thus puffed up, they became incapable of accomplishing their providential office. And so the Father, not wanting that through the fault of one people the others might be lost, sent his Son. Being unrecognized by his own fold, Christ addressed himself to the lost sheep, to the Gentiles, and these people, because of the thickness of the shadows in which they were floundering, have accepted the light. So it is that when a child born in a rich family starts believing that this wealth and these honors are his by right, he waxes proud and his eyes go blind to truth. And so, seeking out someone humble and poor, truth gives itself to him and makes of him its herald.

In short, all creatures, from the smallest to the greatest, who come into the world with similar gifts, undergo a similar ordeal, almost always emerge defeated, and thus delay their real happiness and perfection.

Let us then distrust the charm that emanates from our own qualities; let us get used to distinguishing our immortal self from the instruments loaned to it for the accomplishment of its work. For instance: our body with its strength, dexterity, beauty; the subtle organs through which we experience the delicacies and splendors of nature and of art; the mental faculties that permit us to understand, classify, and direct the energies of matter that elevate us to the serene speculations of the abstract; the energy of will that procures for us such intense joys (intense but dangerous joys of conquest and domination)—none of all this belongs to us. But alas! Even if, theoretically, we know our status as born-debtors, as perpetual borrowers, for all practical purposes we still conduct ourselves as if we were the legitimate proprietors of ourselves. We resemble the Pharisee who, seeing Jesus accept the homage of the courtesan, concludes that he did not realize what she was—we believe in appearances, we judge others from appearances, we respect nothing but appearances.

To distinguish what is transitory from what is permanent is such an important study that all the initiators of Asia have built it as a principle into their systems. It is found at

The Kingdom of Heaven

the heart of Taoism, Brahmanism, Buddhism, Lamaism, and the Sufis of Islam. It is also found in the gospel, but implicitly—rather as a philosophical induction than as a rule of practice. Jesus Christ has us grasp immediately what is concrete, rather than teach us how to think. He prefers to teach us first how to live. It is a fact that all men do not have the aptitude for meditation, but all can see how their brother suffers, and all can come to his aid. Charity is the supreme initiatrix.

There comes a time, however, when you will have to enlighten and clarify some worried and confused minds, so let us try to find out together in what way God, as the only Reality, communicates himself to man, inculcating him with the intimate meaning of illusory appearances.

First of all (though this may seem pretentious) I must try to tell you something about divine Essence, and also about the Trinity, to spare you recourse to the special works of the Fathers of the Church and theologians. Without going into details, I will simply state what I believe, what I hold to be true, what seems to me most comprehensible and least subject to furnishing a pretext to the errors of subjectivism and of pantheism—in short, what seems to me most conformable to the primary idea of Christ.

The Supreme Being is the only totally immaterial Being. As Jesus says to the Samaritan woman: "God is spirit." And since, on another occasion, Jesus declares being one with his Father, I conclude that the Trinity is but an image; doubtless, the best of images, but still an image—for our intelligence, the clearest image of the life of this Supreme Being.

The Supreme Being is one, simple, homogeneous in his essence. He is, if I may say so, independent, free, the sum of all the perfection our sensibility, affectivity, intellect, and

THE HEALINGS OF CHRIST

will can conceive. He is the sum of the infinity of the perfections that the human being will ever be able to conceive. He is the sum of all the possible and all the impossible, of all that has been, of all that is, of all that shall be, of all the before and after, of all duration and of all eternity, of all the finite and infinite, of all the relative and all the absolute. And yet, this immense ensemble forms nothing but the organs and faculties of this Being who in himself is inaccessible to our inquiries.

We can scarcely conceive of a more clear-cut image than that of the activities of God whereby He has wished to come closer to us: I mean the Word. The Word is God: on the one hand, entirely immaterial, free, omnipotent; on the other, entirely material, composed of all varieties of matter (from the densest, such as those of the body, to the more fluidic, such as those of psychism, of mentality, and of will). Because, to my understanding, everything not pure spirit is matter, pure spirit is the only eternal, free substance—sufficient unto itself, developing itself through the sole play of its innate activity—while all other substances (even the most subtle, such as mechanical forces, thought, and will) are subject to laws: they are born, wear out from use, and need other substances in order to continue to exist or to be renovated.

The Word is that part of the Person of God who takes care of Creation: to give it life, preserve its existence, or transfigure its temporal, discontinuous, and provisional existence up to eternal life—that is, up to continuous, lasting and ever-renewed eternal life. During the course of this function the Father gives orders, the Son works; the Spirit is the dual virtue of this command and of its realization. The Father creates, the Son restores, the Spirit saves. But

The Kingdom of Heaven

before all this, the Father has decreed, the Son has furnished living substance to the created being, and the Spirit has organized it in a harmonious manner.

My advice is that the best means to find out what the divine operations are about, is to gather together from the four gospels the passages relating to the work proper to each of the three Persons. Moreover, this search is not difficult, and does not take too long. In any case, it is always preferable to have recourse to the source than to commentaries, and to the original works than to manuals of critics and popularizers.

However, as to our present study, I agree that it is no less difficult to grasp the movement of divine life in the world or in man, than in itself.

Christian tradition prior to St Thomas Aquinas recognizes in the human composite a body, a soul, and a spirit; but it does not define exactly what the soul is, or what the spirit is. Some authors place the spirit above the soul; others place the soul above the spirit. It seems that the general opinion of mystics attributes preeminence to the spirit, and designates it as the seat of the self, under the name of the spirit-proper. Under this hypothesis, regeneration and salvation consist in the obliteration of the spirit-proper and its replacement by the Spirit of God. The perfect man here on earth would be a body and soul saturated by the Holy Spirit, which would infuse the other two principles with all the virtues and wisdom they can receive.

Theologians who study Paul's text that enumerates body (*soma*) the soul (*psyche*), and spirit (*pneuma*),[2] see the sensitive soul or breath as psyche, and the intellectual or supe-

---

[2] I Thessalonians 5:23.

rior soul as pneuma. The work of salvation would then consist of governing the soul so that it never obeys the body and always obeys the Spirit of God. In this way, our body can be acclimatized, through salvation and resurrection, to the kingdom of God. The man who fulfills Christ's precepts, similarly to the wildstock grafted upon the vinestock itself, will gradually cease to draw his life from the world, and draw it from heaven, becoming celestial and spiritual while retaining his regenerated body and soul. The Spirit will unite him to the Word.

We are the image of God in our body and soul. We start resembling that image of God when his Spirit descends into our human nature and transmutes it. When we obey the gospel, God possesses us in the measure wherein each of us is capable of receiving that possession. The Spirit influences our being; and just as the sun through its heat and light permits seeds buried in the earth to grow, so the Spirit through his gifts or graces causes the eternal seed to grow—the seed that, at the very beginning, the Father deposited into our center. This is how the inner Christ grows within us.

The only merit we bring is to show ourselves docile to grace—a docility, naturally, which embraces the most heroic efforts in the struggle against selfishness, and likewise in the struggle to attain brotherly love.

As far as creatures other than man are concerned, it is through our intermediation that heaven acts upon the three physical kingdoms, upon the invisibles, and upon earthly or cosmic forces. Each human being is the center of a little universe which he pulls upward in his ascension or drags down in his fall. Each disciple distributes (albeit almost always unconsciously) to all these non-human creatures whose sun he becomes, the divine life, modulated and

The Kingdom of Heaven

adapted to their various receptivities by its passage through the intellect, the soul, and even the body of that disciple. Hence the gravity of our daily conduct and the weight of our responsibilities.

On the one hand, then, as we become temples of the Spirit, external impurities become more and more incapable of defiling us; on the other hand, and according to the same progression, our eye discerns more and more clearly the true depth of creatures. Take these two consequences to their limit, and you will understand the attitude and the strength of Jesus. We will try (will we not?) to model our intimate being in the image of what we will gradually discover about his soul.

The Flotsam and Jetsam

WHERE RELIGIOUS MORALE is concerned, the faithful have a tenacious tendency to believe that they might become defiled by external contacts. The books of Moses, Manu, and Zoroaster affirm this misconception through the extent of their prescribed rituals. Doubtless, just as foul air contaminates our blood, the proximity of a criminal, the use of certain foods, the frequenting of certain locales contaminates our double and prepares the ground for our psyche to commit errors. Diseases due to psychic causes may be born as the result of the psychical environment, just as living by a swamp or having contact with a leper may cause physical diseases. But this is nature's horizon. The instinct to hate is not a sin; following that instinct is the sin. Cancer is not a sin, but the revolt of the patient against his disease would be a sin. From God's standpoint, there is sin only when one consents fully to any kind of evil solici-

THE HEALINGS OF CHRIST

tation, whether it comes from our self or our non-self—it is born within our innermost center, in our free-will.

Today's moralists heed doctors and psychiatrists. According to these various experts, any infraction of morality is due to one cause only: a physiological disequilibrium. This is not true. As an example, let us take a man whose spiritual path must encounter the demon of murder. We don't need to ask why, because for those of us who are convinced of the Father's justice and goodness, it is enough to know that everyone must undergo the trials of every temptation before entering heaven. If this man, destined to meet murder, did not carry within himself the possibility of becoming a murderer, the trial would have no hold on him; it would be inoperative. As the feeling of immanent justice tells us, he will only face this encounter if there is a moral defect in him, a psychic defect, a physiological defect, thanks to which the demon of murder can cling on him. The morbid disequilibrium of the criminal or of the vice-ridden man is an effect, not a cause. One has only to study the authentic portraits of saints to find in them some of the same stigmatas that our legal medical experts use as loopholes and hold as attenuating circumstances regarding the responsibility of their clients. But whereas the criminal has permitted himself to be ruled by his instinct, the saint has triumphed and transformed his natal vice into a virtue.

Therefore, just as the Pharisee thought, ordinary beings become sullied through outer impurities because they do not fight against the inner attraction that these outer impurities provoke. But the others, the extraordinary beings, the prophets, cannot be sullied. On the contrary, they purify, because they have become impeccable. They have attained mastery over all their physical, mental, and psychic organ-

The Kingdom of Heaven

isms. Ordinary men feed upon bread, meat, greens; or again, upon sensations, feelings, or ideas. All of this is external. The others feed only upon what is internal, drawn from the essences that are truly innermost: those of the pure spirit. Even before having received his complete liberation, the perfect servant of the Father may be fed in his physical body by the spirit, just as his invisible organs are also fed. Mystical life is not limited to our superior regions. In fact, it has the tendency of invading us totally, so that heaven is not just over yonder in the beyond, but right here, as well as there. The will of God must also be accomplished upon all earths, even to the very one from which our body is made. The reign of God must be established upon all planets, in all social states, just as it has to be established within our carnal beings.

Let me stress and further elucidate this matter of the genesis of sin. Our being does not contain everything. Man and the universe are the two halves of one whole. We can perceive, and can conceive, only the things whose counterpart we possess already within us. The child, in whose brain there is an inadequate number of the myriad cells in which mathematical ideas are localized, will not understand anything about algebra. The event that may leave one spectator cold, transports another into a state of furor. That is because the latter carries in his mind the germ of anger, while in the former the germ is lethargic. Likewise for all states of mind, all desires, all sciences, all arts. What constitutes the goodness or badness of an act, then, is my consent to the solicitation coming from outside, or provoked in me by some circumstance. Frequenting a saint does not make me a saint; it disposes me to choose holiness if the seed of it has already been planted within me. To become a saint in

THE HEALINGS OF CHRIST

my turn, I must consent, I must want it. Associating with a criminal does not make me become a criminal; it inclines me toward evil; but, to become a criminal in my turn, I have to consent, I have to want to—or, all too often, alas! it is enough for me to let myself go, because the bad seeds are still more highly developed in me than the good ones.

And so, the courtesan could not sully or soil the Master, who in his turn could not repel her moving repentance.

What a lesson to be learned from his welcome to her! Let us study the circumstances.

We can, in fact, divide the examples Christ gives us into two categories: in the first, everything he proposes we reproduce, according to our strength and under the condition of our complete sincerity; in the second, everything he alone possesses the power and the right to execute, and which we can only do when we have received the baptism of the Spirit.

Even as far as the acts of the first category are concerned, we must take definite precautions, because of our weakness, because of the facility with which we dupe ourselves. For instance, many men of goodwill are imprudent; many, wanting to imitate Jesus, frequent the lower levels of social hells with the goal of seeing hope light up in the lusterless eyes of those souls wallowing in despair, or aiming to revive the notion of morality in the numbed conscience of criminals and perverts. Of course, the intention of these converters is worthy of praise; but how many fail in their generous attempts either because they have counted too much upon their own strength or because, in the mistaken belief that they were fulfilling a fraternal gesture, they were in fact obeying an obscure covetousness from whose insidious promptings they were unable to disentangle themselves. In

The Kingdom of Heaven

either case, they are sadly mistaken both about themselves and about the wretch they were trying to help, for no one is saved by force. Destiny has no pity for our mistakes; only heaven grants its indulgence and mercy.

The philanthropist whose zeal is imprudent, who permits himself to be drawn into the corrupt milieu he aspired to cleanse, faces the rigorous law of causality that obliges him to shoulder later the personal consequences of his failures and, moreover, holds him responsible for the greater falls of the unfortunate whom he attempted to raise from the gutter, but who fell again deeper on account of his weakness.

But let us not err on the side of caution either. If the advancing disciple, the "soldier of Christ," must run ahead of spiritual struggles and risks, any Christian has a duty not to turn his back on the social wrecks he encounters along the way. If the good bourgeois turns away from the vagabond, he is doing a disservice, bringing down upon his own head the fate of the vagabond and the very vices that may have reduced his brother to begging. Other examples naturally spring to mind, but there is no need to go into them.

The "soldier of Christ" is a Christian who has aged like good wine under the mystical harness. He has already put in much effort. He has experience, and when Jesus engages him in his service, he gives him the proper arms. Battle is his business. He must show courage; and for him, recklessness does not exist. Such a man will therefore meet the challenge head-on. He will seek out the hopeless, the defiant, the vicious, the ignorant, the rebellious, the inert, to get them out of their misery; and, if he succumbs in the reckless attempts to which his zeal leads him, the angels rescue him, and Jesus would return to earth for him alone, rather than let him be lost.

THE HEALINGS OF CHRIST

Let us not be surprised, then, at the latitude heaven grants us for our accomplishments; after all, heaven only wants those services we offer from our generous heart and free will. Undoubtedly there is a minimum we have to provide, otherwise we will go backwards on the mystical road. In the case we are dealing with at present, this means never refusing to lend a helping hand to society's outcasts when they ask for it. As to the maximum, it is measureless, because true fraternal love always finds something to give, even when it believes it has given its all. Heaven lets us be the masters of our dedicated services. Christ does not consider his servants as salaried employees; he raises them to the dignity of friends, because he only wants their services when freely rendered, that is, when done for love.

This priceless favor, which he grants us when he admits us to the unbelievable parity of becoming his friends, holds us as obligated. If you feel or see Christ merely as the Master, no matter how good or indulgent you think him to be, then serve him as a servant would; but if you see him as your God, your particular and personal Friend, will it not be necessary for you to respond to this incomprehensibly close bond with his gigantic glory by offering your whole self, by giving the deepest part of your self, by offering an ever-increasing series of sacrifices that will never slake your thirst nor satisfy the ceaseless desires of your charity?

Our mystical duty is therefore to strive for more. "No one is bound to do the impossible," says the common sense of the crowd. But if we are among those servants whom Jesus fulfills by calling them Friends, it is to the impossible that we are bound. This is whither we must strive, and we will live this paradoxical life all the better as we become more intimately humble and forgetful of ourselves.

The Kingdom of Heaven

Divine Love

NOW THAT WE are able to discipline ourselves to some degree, let us make the attempt to love our Master—on the one hand, by holding the beast in us well in hand; on the other, by letting the angel in us spread his wings. The love any creature may feel towards its Creator differs radically from all other kinds of love. In the passions men and women feel, no matter how pure and idealistic we imagine them to be, there is always found at their inception, or in the course of their fulfillment, emanations from the flesh, harmonies from magnetic vibrations that belong to the earthly. Had Beatrice or Vittoria Colonna been shrews, I doubt Dante Alighieri or Michelangelo Buonarroti could have gotten along with them, even within the immaterial confines of art or spirituality.

Love for one's fellow man, if it is not vitalized by the love of God, becomes rather rapidly philanthropy: the industrialization of charity. As far as friendship is concerned, the fact that so many speak of it leads one to believe that no one really knows it. On that subject, Plato seems to me too metaphysical, Cicero too reasonable, Montaigne too individualistic. Friendship between two people can only be an ennobling counterpoint to individualism. When this noble sentiment unites more than two, it enters into the divine order, because collaboration with God becomes necessary to it then, so that our various kinds of invincible selfishness do not kill it.

In short, we cannot engender anything in the idealistic realm if we do not call God to our aid in our exaltations. How then can we love God? When do we love him?

A state of inner plenitude and joy, a state of prayerfulness and optimism, doubtless indicates love for our Master; but often it is only a superficial or outer type of love born out of the happy conjectures in our invisible bodies, which the very first breaths of adversity may extinguish.

When charitable works, ascetic pursuits, and prayer lose their appeal, if we force ourselves to do them, however disgusted we may feel, however certain we may be of their uselessness—that is a more solid and already deeper love of God. Anticlericals believe that the long day and night prayers of contemplative orders merely light the fires of imagination in the souls of monks and nuns (proving thereby that they themselves have never experienced this). On the contrary, these slow psalmodies, breviaries, and rosaries gradually break down the novice's vague ardor, rid him of his pious prejudices, make him see the mystical problem in its simplicity, in its frightening nakedness, dispel his devout romanticism, give free rein to the cold reason and critical sense indispensable for the interior life, and, finally, bring the focus of divine love from the outer regions of the self to increasingly inner centers.

True love of God is engendered through feeling true love for one's fellow man. There are many kinds of compassion. The most common is felt as a physical sensitivity that we must transform into a more intimate, profound, serene sympathy. We must reach the point where we neither see the faults nor the shortcomings of those whom we help, while nonetheless not allowing ourselves to be duped. We must not condemn the unfortunate: in coming to the aid of their personal needs and helping them with their earthly destiny, we must see them as part of the body of our Christ.

By adoring her Master publicly, Mary Magdalene recognized those things that were as yet unrevealed. Her magnif-

The Kingdom of Heaven

icent heart grasped the very mystery of God's rapport with his creature, and it is because of this that her love became the seed of the future ecstasies of all contemplatives—each of whom, even now, is united to the Lord according to his strength. The greatest things always take their start from a very small incident.

The Faith That Saves

WERE A CREATED BEING able to receive the plenitude of one word of Jesus, he would in an instant be transported to heaven; even while on earth, he would enjoy perfect peace, total faith, and final salvation. We can only hear some of the echoes of the Word; and owing to this incapacity of ours, Jesus can only offer us, and we can only grasp, an intermittent peace, a salvation hoped for (even though it is certain), because our faith is partial, discontinuous, inadequate.

Jesus teaches brotherly love first, along with the love of God. These two inseparable loves permit the realization of all the projects of providence; they satisfy the desires, fulfill the needs, of all beings, and in due time bring them all together to their supreme accomplishments. Our very good Father thus orders the course of the universe, because we are less incapable of loving than of believing. So, Jesus, whose maxims all imply faith, only names it in certain cases relating to the idea of salvation, such as those dealing with illness, accident, or spiritual blindness. Moreover, if, to love God, it is essential to first believe in him, to clarify and strengthen this initially nebulous belief, we must compel the self to serve him out of love, through concrete acts, every day more than the day before, every hour more than the hour before. In the religious order, faith and charity are

THE HEALINGS OF CHRIST

inseparable because they are the dual aspects of love: love of God and love for men. The catechistic doctrine then adds hope. I would venture to say that the true disciple, the soldier of Christ, does not need hope.

What would he hope for? his own salvation? Is it not certain that his Father can fulfill his most audacious aspirations in an instant? The salvation of others? Does not his faith give him assurance in that respect? Were he to be deprived of the solace of visions, of the splendor of ecstasies, of the simple sustenance of common prayer; were he lacking the kind of intelligence that consoles through the certainties of a doctrine; were he to be confined in the darkest of nights—his faith would still affirm and reiterate the constant presence of his Master. That would suffice.

A scientist who during his research finds the same phenomena repeated again and again attains some certainty regarding that fact. But faith is certitude of something unseen, of something one does not understand, something that logic would prove to be impossible. As long as this certainty has not invaded sufficiently vast territories within us, it does not give us the strength to conduct ourselves according to the absurdity of antiquated wisdom, and it is only a shadow of true faith. Thus, one can say, strictly speaking, that no one on earth knows what faith is, since the one who would possess faith the size of "a mustard seed" would be obeyed by all of physical nature.

In the kindergarten of the school of faith (and we are merely at that level) we are often misled by illusions. The desires of our heart, no matter how sincerely they seem to gush and spark forth, do not set our whole being ablaze in an instant. It takes time, a great deal of time, for this fire to burn away all that is putrid and arid within us. Several con-

The Kingdom of Heaven

temporary playwrights and writers have recently gained renown for having discovered that there are in us not only two opposite tendencies, but a large number of incoherent personalities whose complex discords help to explain the bizarre quirks of our conduct (no matter what our background or education may have been) when we are in the throes of a passionate crisis. This is not at all a new discovery: psychologists of old, now scorned, have described such outbursts.

For instance, let us take a new convert, transfigured by the certainties he has received, who from the depths of his youthful enthusiasm consecrates himself to God. This Christian, still ignorant of the complexities of his enterprise, sincerely imagines having given himself definitively and wholly to God and that, subject to a watchful surveillance, everything will go steadily along. Alas, no! His whole person is a battlefield wherein more than two adversaries are fighting—there are thousands. To state that we are flesh and spirit is putting it rather too simply. Each cell of our body possesses its own will. Each bone, each blood vessel, each muscle, each nerve, each physiological plexus, has a will of its own. Each of the senses, each feeling, each mental faculty, each intellectual facet peculiar to each branch of speculative or practical activity, also has its own will. What is more, the enormous unconscious, of which physiological consciousness is only a small part, has its own general will and innumerable particular wills that govern the immaterial organs, secret functions, and unknown powers that together make up the invisible man. And the aforementioned consciousness registers only the smallest fraction of these myriad wills to whose outcome the still imperfect nervous system can be sensitive.

Hence, our said convert is affiliated with God only by a few points of his being. This is essential, and suffices to assure the mystical *grand-oeuvre* at a later date. But there are, in him, millions of other points that for the time being do not feel God. Some do not feel him yet, others do not feel him anymore. The former must be educated, the latter must be re-educated. That is what moral rules, ascetic disciplines, examination of conscience, meditation, and prayer are for. You will understand how essential it is for the disciple to bring his pious impulses to fruition, to govern his impulses according to the ideal, to become master of himself, master of his body and senses, master of his intellect, and above all, master of his passions.

Thus the majority of Christians possess a faith of sentiment sufficient for them to conduct themselves, at times, according to the standards of heaven; others, whose intelligence is more demanding, make use of this soul disposition to reinforce their conviction with the solid reasoning of theology; those who score a success, however, subjecting their instincts, tastes, words, opinions, and actions to the inflexible rule of the plenary faith Christ proposes to us—these are quite rare. For that, the disciple would have to keep an ever-watchful eye on all his inner reflexes and all external inputs, and confront them every second with the ideal of faith, then forcibly conform them to it, for the smallest things as well as for the most important. Such a continuous and pitiless discipline is impossible to realize, primarily because the perfect mastery over the self it demands is the very problem to be solved—the culture of the will demands time. Moreover, to discern in our motives what incites us towards faith, or away from faith, one would have to possess living knowledge—which happens to be one of the results of faith.

The Kingdom of Heaven

For example, when we are on the street, all of a sudden an idea strikes us to cross over to the other side. We may reject this capricious desire. But, if we cannot discern its secret motive, how will we ever discover whether by remaining on one sidewalk or by crossing over to the other, we have or have not followed an act of faith?

We are complex beings. Only in geometry is the straight line the shortest way from one point to another. In the moral world, as in life, the shortest road is often quite winding. So, the Father, who desires our being able to receive complete faith one day, now recommends charity.

The shadows of eternal love saturate this perishable universe far more than do the shadows of faith. Let us continue our little story, supposing that our disciple moves, no longer towards faith, but towards charity. The possible causes of his desire to cross the street will then be reduced to two: to avoid inconvenience, or to procure pleasure; to cause inconvenience to others, or to offer them help. Then he will decide, choosing either the least pleasant itinerary or the one that gives him more. The rule of charity is much clearer for us, as we are now.

Psychological awareness and moral awareness function as the two poles of the self. The self, the "I," egoism, individualism, egotism, howsoever it may be called, is everything to us, the principle of all the obstacles to our spiritual advancement. It is as opposed to charity as doubt is to faith, as discouragement is to hope.

But doubt is already outside the realm of egoism. It is a lack of self-confidence or a vanity of the intellect. While anyone can make out the difference between a selfish tendency and an altruistic one, to go after doubt and conquer it demands broader experience. To do battle against the

THE HEALINGS OF CHRIST

ego, all you have to do is say "No." If, to chase way doubt, you resort to reason, you reinforce the doubt; and simply denying it requires wills already very robust.

In the dissociation of the mysterious divine unity that (so that we may understand it better) is presented to us as the dogma of the Trinity, faith belongs to the Father, peace to the Son, and salvation to the Holy Spirit. The practice of charity spiritualizes the self, which then becomes capable of perceiving the unrevealed when it presents itself before the self under one of the forms of the Word; and with the light from the Consoler, the self receives pacification.

Everyone lives by some kind of faith; one believes in his business, another in his art, another in friendship, another in some theory—even the sceptic believes in his scepticism. Yet, all these beliefs, from the most vulgar to the finest, from base materialism to the most impersonal, reach their limit someday.

And this "someday," which those who live it say is a death—this someday is in reality the happy dawn of deliverance and rebirth. Human beings are an ungrateful lot. When this faith, which for so many days gave them the strength to live, collapses within them, they insult and curse it. They should bless it. As long as they refuse the Immutable, are they not condemning themselves to mutation? Why do they cherish phantoms and neglect the living?

Without doubt, the strong assurance that sustains the artist through his anxious struggles, that imparts to the thinker the serene patience of disinterestedness, disappoints far less than the ephemeral triumphs of fortune or of fame. The truly representative poets, painters, scientists, and philosophers command respect. But which one among these, unless he has lived as a Christian, will be able to testify at

The Kingdom of Heaven

his last hour that he dies certain of having reached his ideal? Naturally, this determination or will that no defeat ever breaks is one of the highest nobilities in man; but it gives him such a bitter, dry, and ofttimes denuded happiness that only dogged souls can be satisfied with it. But if our ideal is God, his closeness brings us a joy that is alive, harmonious, human, opulent, accessible to everyone; and it alone makes us capable of fraternizing with all forms of life,

Without mystical faith, the most formidable mover and shaker gathers but fleeting clouds, the most sublime painter captures but one of eternal beauty's shadows, the deepest thinker conceives but one reflection of eternal truth. With mystical faith, the humblest services, the most menial of tasks, become transfigured, and their fruits ripen under the sun of pure spirit.

Before becoming convictions, the various faiths of men rise up as vocations. Each of us, even before birth, is called simultaneously by gods and God. We listen more readily to the voice of the gods because they dwell in the envelopes of the earth, and because our heart inhabits one of these envelopes also—whereas, because the Word stands in the center of the world, outside us, and at the center of our self, we do not hear him very well.

Were the artist to heed the call from God, he would become that much more sensitive to the call of beauty—do not his anxieties prove his powerlessness? And would he not find measureless help in the enrichments the angels would bring to his still incomplete sensitivity, to his often unilateral thought, to his technique so linked to and limited by his temperament? If only the inventor, philosopher, and scientist would heed the call from God, conforming their life to the standard of heaven and ceaselessly steering their

THE HEALINGS OF CHRIST

research and meditations back into the axis of eternity, would they not perceive possibilities as yet unperceived by them, discover ideas till now foreign to their spirit, and undergo crucial and decisive experiences? Well, of course! Because since the time of Jesus, whoever works for him succeeds by him.

Salvation is not just for later and beyond worlds, because God is not just up-there or over-there. Since the time of Jesus Christ, God is now and down-here. There is a divine Presence for all creatures who have brought their immediate cosmic work to a close; there is also a divine Presence for those beings still laboring on the path. There is a divine Presence in the fields as well as in the office. There is one for the workman as for the farmer, for the father, mother, and child. There is one for mathematicians, chemists, astronomers; one for industrialists, merchants, administrators; one for prince and citizen; one for monk, soldier, sailor. In short, every person on this earth or in other fields whose shimmer fills the nights, every man and woman is born able to glimpse this Presence, to understand, to love, to imitate one of the forms of the eternal Word, one of the facets of Our Lord Jesus Christ.

But not one of these billions of beings will ever see the august Face unless he heeds its call, unless he strains to have faith, because faith comes through understanding. Let him listen; let him force himself to hear. History does not yet show us any of the geniuses who illuminate its avenues as having had the strength to exercise this tyranny over the self completely. None, since, alas, in the character of these most illustrious, one can still discover flaws!

In pointing out weak spots on these magnificent torches, I do not want to distract your admiration. We must love

The Kingdom of Heaven

these men, all of them, and take from each the lesson we are capable to receiving from them.

St Paul as well as da Vinci, St Augustine as well as Goethe, Homer as well as Rabelais, Montaigne as well as Corneille, Shakespeare as well as Michelangelo, St Ignatius of Loyola as well as Baudelaire, St Vincent de Paul as well as Napoleon, St Thomas as well as St Francis—all are to be looked upon as torches on the path leading to the supreme Ideal, the Archetype, the source and end of all particular ideals—the path, that is, to Jesus Christ.

And above all, you have to want to do better than these giants. This is not a paradox. However weak we may be, in the eyes of the Father, we can become greater than the greatest of men, if we better realize the possibilities received from his hands. This is the work of faith.

So, we must continue to grasp the words of Jesus, even the simplest of them, in their total sense and also in their most personal sense; to apply them to the past and to the future, but most of all to the present, to the immediate moment. Any act, any state of soul, experienced according to true faith gives the peace of Christ and his salvation to the part of us that has acted according to his word. The faith that he proposes we follow comprises all natural and human faiths—or rather, these are nothing but the inverted shadows of that faith. The crowd lives in those shadows. Doubtless, so do we; but we possess the power of living in the midst of this crowd of phantoms with a secret light, in peace and in his love. The day is coming when reality will invade everything through an immense cataclysm that will be the salvation of the world and the salvation of all created beings.

THE HEALINGS OF CHRIST

The Function of Faith

PISTIS OR FIDES are the words classical antiquity used to designate "belief"—hence the many New Testament passages where these terms signify intellectual adherence as well as sentimental attachment to the Christic concept. Secular Christian usage has enriched the meaning of these beautiful words.

For the Catholic, faith is an intellectual assent under the command of the will (St Thomas). For the Protestant, faith is a moral fact, a certain state of soul preceded by assent and followed by obedience (Hastings). "I trust in the wisdom and truthfulness of God. I admit and accept his word"—such is the Catholic act of faith. In order to have faith, the Protestant believes that, as a result of this belief, there must be born in me a feeling of abandonment to God, of certainty of his support, of humility, of confidence in his mercy.

Catholics and Protestants are in agreement on the necessity of having trust in God and in the merits of Jesus Christ in order to obtain pardon, and on the impossibility, without this pardon, of atoning for the evil one has committed. On the other hand, Protestants believe that pardon and salvation are certain and assured, provided one has this trust in faith, and that without it none can be saved. The Council of Trent accepts neither of these two propositions.

The Apostle to the Gentiles gives us the definition of faith (Hebrews 11:1), of which many different translations have been given us. It seems to me quite essential to list them here.

Here are three Catholic translations:

> Faith is the substance (or the reality, or a firm expectation, according to some ecclesiastics) of things one

The Kingdom of Heaven

hopes for, a conviction (or a demonstration) of those one does not perceive. (Abbé Crampon)

Est autem fides sperandum substantia rerum, argumentum non apparentium. (Vulgate)

Faith is the support of the things we hope for, the evidence of those we do not see. (Father Amelote)

Here are some Protestant translations:

Faith is having a definite confidence in what we hope for, and a non-doubt in what we do not see. (Luther)

Faith is a supporting wall of the things one hopes for and a certification of those one does not see. (Bible of Gabriel Brun, 1586)

Faith is a definite assurance of the things one hopes for, a conviction of the things one sees not. (Menegoz)

Faith is a living representation of the things one hopes for, and a demonstration of those one does not see. (Osterwald)

Faith is a firm assurance of the things one hopes for, a demonstration of those one sees not. (Synodal Version)

Faith is a firm awaiting of the things one hopes for, a demonstration of those one sees not. (Segond)

Faith is a conviction relative to what one hopes for, and a certitude regarding facts one does not see. (Reuss)

Faith is the firm conviction of things one hopes for, the absolute certitude of facts one does not see. (Stapfer)

THE HEALINGS OF CHRIST

In order to really understand St Paul's thought, let us note here that to have faith, so that it may live, he adds love (charity) along with works (Galatians 5:6; I Corinthians 13:13). If we refer at the same time to the words of Christ, who makes salvation depend on faith (John 3:16), obedience to God's law (Matthew 19:16), the help of grace (John 6:44; 15:5), penance (Matthew 4:17; Mark 1:15), baptism (John 3:5; Mark 16:16), and perseverance (Matthew 10:22), we can logically conclude that salvation requires the combined resources of divine mercy, our intuitive powers, our intellectual faculties, our emotional strength, and our physical energy; in short, God and the whole of man.

Let us also consult the commentators of Christ, the theologians.

St Basil (*Homelia de Fide*) defines faith as a disposition through which we believe in the revealed truths of God. St John Chrysostom declares: "Faith consists in believing in that which one does not see, and to trust ourselves to the authority of the one who made the promise." (*In Genesim*, chap. 6, hom. 36) The same conception of a dogmatic faith dominates the Apostle's Creed known as that of St Athanasius, composed either in Gaul or Spain during the fourth or fifth century, as well as the doctrine of St Augustine (*de utilitate credenti; de fide rerum quae non videntur; de videndo Deo*) and of his disciple St Fulgence (*de fide ad Petrum*).

St Thomas (*Summa*, second part, questions 1 to 15) considers faith as follows:

> Faith's formal aim or motif of credibility is primal truth, which means God; its material aim is what the faithful believe. The truths upon which faith is based have been divided into several articles and set forth in

The Kingdom of Heaven

the Apostles' Creed. To believe means to adhere firmly to the revealing word. The act of faith is meritorious. The habit of faith, as regards faith itself, has been defined in the Epistle to the Hebrews (11:1): "Faith is that which gives substance our hopes, the demonstration (or the conviction) of what we do not see." It is the first of the virtues, has the intellect as its subject, and is the most certain of the intellectual virtues. The habit of faith was established in the angels before their glorification, it is in demons who are obliged to believe in the revealed word that is transmitted by the Church, but it is only in men subject to the condition that they accept all the articles of the Apostle's Creed. The succor of supernatural essence offered us to enable us to embrace divine truth is that of grace.

Faith has the effect of producing in us the fear of being separated from God. The gifts corresponding to faith are: the gift of intellect and the gift of knowledge which, being more speculative than practical, helps us to discern what we must believe or not believe. The vices opposite to faith are infidelity, blasphemy, ignorance, and the lack of intelligence. Ancient law did not possess any precept concerning faith; one had to be established in the New Law.

Thus, faith, viewed in the Catholic sense, is not a purely intellectual act, but an act where the will influences the intelligence. An act through which we believe in a dogma presupposes a move of the soul towards God. Hence it may have a moral and religious value, as well as an initial salutary value. That is why St Thomas states that "the first union of the soul with God is done through faith" and that "the first principle of the purification of the heart is faith, which takes away the impurity of error; after which, if faith is perfected through charity, it produces perfect purification." Although faith-belief is inferior to charity, it still has the right of priority, for the order of psychological development one goes from the imperfect to the perfect. Thus for man, faith-belief is the doorway to Christianity. It lays a foundation for, and sustains, the other acts of virtue. It inaugurates justification, then consummates it with hope and charity.

The Council of Trent defines faith as "believing that a thing is true." "Faith, unless it is joined together with hope and charity, does not unite one perfectly with Christ, and does not make one a living member of his body." (*can.* 8, *n.* 800) However: "it is a true faith, though it be not a live faith; and he who has faith without charity is a Christian." (*can.* 28, *nn.* 8–38) "Faith is the beginning of the salvation of man..." (*can.* 8. *n.* 801) So "anathema to anyone who claims that the ungodly is justified by faith alone," meaning that nothing else is required or cooperates to obtain the grace of justification.

The Council of the Vatican defines: "By this faith that is the beginning of the salvation of man, the Catholic Church intimates a supernatural virtue through which... we believe what is stated in divine revelation to be true." (*sess.* 3, *canon* 3) Further: "Faith is a supernatural virtue by which, helped and warned by the grace of God, we hold as true that which was revealed." (*Cocile Vatican: Const. Dei Filius*, chap. 3)

In sum: the Scriptures and the organs of tradition suppose or teach that faith is an adhesion of the spirit to revealed dogmas.

Let us now see what the Reformation says.

Calvin keeps to the concept of an intellectual faith. But

The Kingdom of Heaven

in certain passages (notably *Christian Institution*, I, IV, chap. 1) he introduces a mystical element: "We obtain salvation . . . insofar as we recognize the Father as being our benevolent Father for the reconciliation that has been made by Christ, and because we accept Christ as having been given us in justice, sanctification, and life." During the 17th and 18th century, Protestant theology as a whole oscillates between the intellectualistic and the mystical tendencies. At the beginning of the 19th century, some English missionaries gave preeminence to idea over sentiment, bringing the movement back to orthodoxy. Schleiermacher (d. 1834) teaches that religion consists essentially in the life of the heart, or in sentiment. Samuel Vincent, pastor of Nîmes, says: "The known-quantities of faith are simple and nondiscursive; they are not the offshoot of the play of our intellectual faculties." (*Du protestantisme en France*, 1829) For him, Christianity is much less a doctrine than a way of life, and he separates the gospel from scholastic symbols.

Then comes Alexandre Vinet (d. 1847), who affirms that faith is "purely an inner view upon the truths of salvation, a communion of the heart with truth, a way of life rather than a particular view." (*Étude sur Blaise Pascal*). For Scherer and Colani, faith, again, is a moral act that consists in a union with Jesus Christ. (Scherer: *Revue théologique*, 1850, vol. 1, 55 ff; 1551, vol. 3, 98 ff; Colani: 1351, vol. 3, 1 ff) For Auguste Bouvier, faith is "the gift of one's thought and one's heart to the God of the gospel, and the union of one's soul with Jesus Christ," and theology is "the manner of translating this sentiment engendered by the gospel into ideas, into systematic concepts." (J.-E. Roberty: *Auguste Bouvier. Protestant Theologian*, Paris, Alcan, 89)

Liberal Protestantism then began to distinguish between

THE HEALINGS OF CHRIST

faith and beliefs: Eugene Menegoz (*Publications diverses sur le fidéisme et son application à l'enseignement chrétien traditionnel,* 3 vols: Paris, Fischbacher, 1909); and his *Réflexions sur l'Évangile du Salut* (Paris, Fischbacher, 1879) even goes so far as to admit the salvation of a man who would deny the existence of Christ, provided that his "heart be warm enough to give itself entirely to God." (vol. 1, 274) But Menegoz recognizes that faith does encompass an intellectual element: a belief that plays the role of an active element in the formation of mystical faith. In any case, man is saved by faith, by repentance, and by the gift of his heart to God, no matter what his beliefs, his errors, or his heresies. The believer is saved uniquely by faith, by the consecration of his soul to God—independently of his theories and of his opinions.

In this system, the Christian faith does not differ substantially from that of Islam or Buddhism; both, in fact, feel lifted above the sensible world by the speculations of thought, and are attached to God by a veritable embrace. Here, faith is the gift of the heart, a communion with God; dogma is nothing but the envelope of belief. Faith is immutable; dogma varies. We consider scriptural doctrines to be the momentary expression of an experience; we express them differently or deny them, while declaring ourselves spiritually in agreement with the sacred writers!

Auguste Sabatier, founder of "Symbolism," situates himself as having the same viewpoint as the creator of "Fideism." Faith is religious feeling, and as it tends to express itself in formulas, it seeks the help of anthropomorphisms or symbols, without giving them any sense of fixity. Hence, in faith one finds a permanent element plus a transitory element. Fideism is particularly attached to the permanent

The Kingdom of Heaven

element, while symbolism rests upon the transitory element. (See particularly: *Esquisse d'une philosophie de la religion d'après la psychologie et l'histoire*, Paris, Fischbacher, 1897; *La doctrine de l'expiation et son évolution historique*, Paris, Fischbacher, 1903. *Les religions d'autorité et la religion de l'esprit*, Paris, Fischbacher, 1905.)

"To be religious, it is not necessary to believe in God in the traditional sense of the word. Everyone who consecrates himself inwardly, and who subjects himself to his law, to the ideal law of humanity, whether he likes it or not, makes an act of religious faith in the exact measure of the energy and the sincerity of this consecration." (*Religions d'autorité*, 493)

And so, fideism paved the path to religious agnosticism. Theodore Flournoy writes: "Faith and autosuggestion are necessarily synonymous." ("Observations de Psychologie religieuse," *in Archives de Psychologie*, vol. 2, 133, Geneva, Oct. 1903) All objects of belief are relegated to the mysterious domain of the unknowable, and reason must abdicate its pretensions of grasping them.

In short, Catholic doctrine proclaims that faith is an assent of the spirit to immutable and revealed truths; the spirit accepts them, not because it sees them, but because God teaches it. Faith is in essence voluntary. It certainly implicates an intellectual element, but if this becomes individualistic and rejects tradition, it introduces into faith the variability of its vicissitudes. Hence agnosticism, in which the act of faith is devoid of the character of obligation. What, indeed, is an act that results from an "infinitely variable element," as Flournoy calls it? It is as much a lie as it is a truth, since what is currently true will soon become false! Hence this rationalism in religious matters, which today

THE HEALINGS OF CHRIST

increases the number of non-Catholic spiritualists who disbelieve in the absolute divinity of Jesus Christ. Hence the modernism that treats faith as a mere sentiment of the heart, without intellectual discipline, and soon without moral discipline. In condemning modernism, the Holy See has safeguarded the precious, irreplaceable notion of Jesus Christ, the only-begotten Son of God, made flesh and risen from the dead.

What is the function of faith in our work for salvation? The controversy between Catholics and Protestants unfolds in the following texts:

> It is through faith in Jesus Christ, not by obeying the law, that a man is justified. (Gal. 2:16)
>
> Man is justified by works and not by faith alone. (James 2:24)

St Paul also adds: "I may have utter faith, so that I can move mountains; yet if I lack charity, I count for nothing. (Cor. 13:3); to which is added: "Meanwhile, faith, hope, and charity persist, all three; but the greatest of them all is charity." (Cor. 13:13) And lastly: "Once we are in Christ, circumcision means nothing, and the want of it means nothing; the faith that finds its expression in love is all that matters." (Gal. 5:6)

Elsewhere the same apostle writes: "A man's faith is reckoned virtue in him." (Rom. 4:5) Faith *per se* is not the totality of conditions necessary to salvation—but God gives us the grace, through Christ, of holding it as sufficient to salvation. If one believes that Christ is God and that he alone can take us to the kingdom of God, this conviction, which our will imposes upon our reason, also imposes itself as a brake to our selfish tendencies, and imposes itself as a

The Kingdom of Heaven

stimulant to our laziness—and this will break open our apertures to the rays of grace, and render our regeneration possible.

According to Paul, the intelligence of the Christian says: "I do not understand, but I accept." The heart of the believer embraces the divine Person of the Savior and loves him; the body of the believer submits to performing the works that the intelligence transported beyond space and time, together with the heart transported into perfect love, command it to do.

What Paul calls works of the law are deeds accomplished through fear, or self-interest, whereas works of faith are those deeds whose motives are supernatural—that is, works of charity, of love. St James and St Paul are, really, perfectly in accord. James never ceases writing that patience, the faculty of suffering a long time without complaints, is a proof of faith, but that it has to be accompanied by perfect works. (James 1:3-4) He does not fail to point out that there is an element of intellectual belief in faith; but that faith, if reduced to this element, as it is with demons (James 2:14), is incomplete and sterile. When reading the Epistles, we must remember that St Paul is addressing the Gentiles, unbelievers, who think they are saved by formal observances; he therefore teaches them the virtue of faith, purification, the spiritualization of motives. On the other hand, James addresses himself to formalistic, ritualistic Jews. He shows them the necessity of realizing that their precepts are dead, and that they must bring them back to life. Both Paul and James want the possibility and the certitude of eternal salvation to enter into the soul of their listeners. Paul assures this salvation via the perfect and total act of the inner man, whose selfsame perfection outweighs the activity of all good, material works; to him, perfect works are the normal and spontaneous fruits of this mystical union made in faith and in love. James, for his part, assures the same salvation through the perfection of works, which implies the perfection of faith; he would advise working for God alone, as faith would follow after.

One must not forget that Paul was an intellectual, a philosopher, initiated into Jewish esotericism. James, being much more of a realist, preferred asceticism and practical effort. James is more concerned with man; Paul is more concerned with God.

In short, when the convert looks at God, it is possible that the Father may judge him as being capable of seeing only Buddha or Muhammad, or the Bab; or perhaps even a Christ scaled down to the level of human imagination. But if the Father judges him capable of perceiving the true Christ, the illumination that then occurs will enlighten either his intellect, his will, or his heart. Thus, this convert will from then on understand either Paul, James, or even Jesus himself. There is no room for disagreement in sacred texts, only incomprehension on the part of the reader, owing either to his lack of intelligence or to his pride.

Moreover, what proof have we that the apostles were unaware of the difference between temporary paradises and eternal bliss? Among the many mysteries Jesus communicated to them, and of which no account has come down to us, do you not think he made them understand that the work of salvation is almost always a secular undertaking? That only if we dedicate ourselves to God now, here on earth, will we be able to realize this vow within the full reach of our personality—in all our concepts, all our feelings, all our acts? Whether or not we accept purgatory,

The Kingdom of Heaven

doesn't the uncertainty of the mode of duration that governs this place bring the imagination into close contact with systems comprising a plurality of existences? And so, let the convert begin the enterprise of his salvation with works whose radiance will open up his inner apartments to light. Let him begin it with the construction of a system of thought, such as Thomism, for example, as a result of which he will be logically inclined to the love of God and to charitable works. Let him begin it, finally, by setting his heart ablaze, which will exalt his intelligence to the threshold of the Unrevealed, and infuse his body with the courage to bear all labors, for the service of his neighbor. Can we not see that this enterprise of salvation, like all journeys, has its beginning, its middle, and its end?

The first step may be undertaken through hope, or rather by the desire for hope, by the need for faith, by carnal pity (which is the beginning of charity); but the intermediate steps, and the last step, is faith, hope, and charity, all three united, all three working together, all giving the pilgrim the strength of taking these steps. Moreover, the greatest servants of God are never more than a step away from the start. So it is that, when this common sense functions on the basis of humility, and upon the habit of carrying out Christic precepts, the meditations of the most pious and wisest of men always reach the same conclusions as those of good, common sense. Whether we begin by understanding or by loving or by acting, the exercise of one of these three functions inevitably carries along and enhances the other two. And so, a sincere man should never have the least fear about his spiritual future. As seen through the light of Jesus Christ, all things are simple and certain.

THE HEALINGS OF CHRIST

Divine Clairvoyance

SO, IN THE EPISODE of the repentant courtesan, we can find the actual fruit of our own experience, whether the hard payments for faults that seem like peccadilloes, or the happiness so strong that it follows pessimistic periods, or this spiritualization of the self that refines our senses and our judgment, or this more permanent intimacy with Christ, or these material failures that force us face to face with our powerlessness, or this slow and secret recovery of our whole being that leads us towards the solid homogeneity of being one with our true Friend.

The further I go, the more I find that the simplest, most direct, most evident statements are the richest in substance. Thus, in the anecdote I am reminding you of, the overriding fact is that Jesus alone discerns the true feelings of the courtesan. Among the witnesses, some are scandalized, others deplore such evident waste—or rather, they do not understand. Jesus alone knows what consumes this woman, what her gesture, so badly interpreted, really means. But our poor eyes, still so weak, have yet to catch a glimpse of such sharpness. It is true that the eye is the mirror of the soul. All we do, all we think, does enter into our eyes. I share my purse, I quell my anger, I excuse a fault, I do anything that confirms the divine commandment: each of these little forces, human at the moment of their outward emission, the Holy Spirit (descending to the rescue of my good will) then integrates, sublimates, into my soul. And from this center they radiate upon my various organisms and spiritualize them. In the same way, but in the opposite direction, faults materialize me; and all the long secret work, whether towards Light or towards Darkness, ends up in the eyes, giving them clarity or opaqueness.

The Kingdom of Heaven

The soul exercises of initiates do nothing but render the nervous system more sensitive to vibrations different from those of the physical plane—but they are still and always dependent upon the general laws of this world. The mystical exercises—prayer, charity, humility—open us to the action of the Spirit, the free agent of all laws. Created forces, even the highest, are spent when they are used; external recovery is indispensable for them. The Spirit, on the contrary, feeds himself from himself, and the more he spends his force, the more his force increases. So, if we dispose the only one of our organs capable of assimilating it—our heart of Light—we need not worry about any details; provided that our conduct remains in the rectitude of Christ, outwardly as well as inwardly, the Spirit will bring us all of heaven, since he is the bond of the Father and the Son. He will heal us morally as well as physically. He will increase life in and about us. He will render all forms of life outside us intelligible to us, because he is love, the very essence of eternal life. But, though he will do all these things, yet he will do so while respecting our little liberty, because he is perfect liberty, Not only will he respect the central liberty of our heart yearning for the light, but he will respect also all the other little individual liberties of our judgment, of our memory, of each of our mental faculties, of our faculties proper to each science, to each art, to each material or soul realization. Finally, he will respect each of the little liberties of each of our corporeal organs, down to the microscopic ones.

That is the reason why the ardor of our desires does not immediately procure for us the privilege to see God. We are not just souls. We are several souls, several spirits, several bodies, and hundreds of parts in each of our three centers:

we are a world. And when the self wills (in order to attain the object of its desire), it is necessary that the greater part of all the energies through which the self operates desire along the same line. Though a king may be an autocrat, in order for him to achieve a conquest it is essential to him that the greater number of his subjects want the same.

Thus, time is necessary to our spiritualization. The courtesan was born with a heart thirsting for the absolute, an intellect desiring perfect beauty, a soul and body desiring perfect happiness. Did her future Master take hold of her during her adolescence and thrust her suddenly upon the road of heaven? No. He first let her drink the cup of deceptions to the dregs. That woman's intelligence had to realize the emptiness of all systems, just as her soul had need to die to all terrestrial joys. And the depth of her falls provided the impetus for the altitude of her future exaltations.

One can find a great many applications to this anecdote of Magdalene at the home of the Pharisee. The following is one such application relative to intellectual civilization.

The essential soul of any being, individual, race, people, planet, science, or art, is one of the modes of the Word. Within this mode of the Word, the personal spirit of each of these creatures possesses its legitimate spouse. But this spouse is also constantly tempted by a courtesan, who is the infernal ferment of greedy egoism that drives the creature towards the cult of the ego or towards material pleasures. Thus, Greek culture, so delicately beautiful, so rich and serene, is the concubine of the white race, whose legitimate bride is the gospel doctrine.

And so, to the courtesan there always comes the moment of repentance. She then throws at the feet of her Master the fruits of her prostitutions, treasures that rationalistic men,

The Kingdom of Heaven

such as Judas, deplore seeing squandered. But this loss is apparent only on the surface, for all of this precious beauty shed at the feet of the Word is transmuted at that very moment into pure, eternal, living Light. And it is one of the most powerful miracles the beloved Healer can perform.

Thus is the existence of the disciple a continuous sequence of deaths and rebirths. Thus does each of his vigorous efforts end in a prostration at the feet of the Beloved, who raises him to his heart. And because of this close and mystical embrace, the disciple then perceives in the gaze of his Friend, in a line of his face, in the fold of his robe, the long-sought light that reveals to him the power, the science, or art that he has passionately striven to possess for so long.

This explains why a change of heart is quite another thing from what one sees on the surface: all the struggles, relapses, persuasive words, are no more than a "boiled-down" version of the vast inner drama in which hundreds of actors are performing. An ordinary man can only play the part of an extra. The one given charge of this conversion directs everything, is everywhere, has a hand in everything. But such a man had first to hoist himself to the Spirit. From then on, everything becomes possible to him. He can regenerate a soul as easily as he can a rock or planet. I am telling you this only to let you know that we are never alone, that divine help always comes at the very instant our resistance is about to surrender.

I have given a good many details regarding Magdalene in order to indicate to you, though summarily, with what profound attention we must read the gospel, how it must be scrutinized with love, how tightly we must unite ourselves to its spirit, so that we may find in the simplicity of its verses the grandiose universes that move freely in them.

Contemplate the multiple repercussions, in space and time, of the actions of a bearer of the Absolute. Without repeating the recriminations of today's feminists about the slavery to which women were once reduced, look at the occult significance of this anecdote.

Jesus, that day, welcomed all the repentances of future sinners, whose erratic images had been evoked by the alternating voices of repentance and love, and were crowding at that moment, at that hour, into the secondary atmosphere of the hall of this Pharisaic banquet.

The laborer acts upon matter only by means of his muscular force; the better-educated engineer's machine does the same work by means of a lever. Likewise, in the Invisible, the ordinary man acts only with the help of rites, practices, or formulas; and even then, the results he obtains are always superficial and precarious. But he to whom the Father has communicated an arcanum can instantly and effortlessly work miracles even more wonderful than the renovation of a heart.

What Are Parables For?

THIS MODE of teaching is one of the most ancient, most popular, and most comprehensible. These similitudes full of imagery, these analogies extracted from daily events, contain in fact a part of truth that either increases or decreases according to the power of attention in the beholder's eye. Let us remember as well that we are held accountable for everything that has been given us to understand, to see, or to hear.

Even the disciples themselves did not immediately comprehend the complete meaning in the discourses of Jesus. It

The Kingdom of Heaven

is only after they had received the gift of tongues that they found, in the words of their Master, what was useful to them for the accomplishment of their mission.

And so, heaven gives some people intelligence, either because they once worked for it, or because they have an action to take in their turn. As for other people, they have to show their good will by trying their best. Besides, we should naturally understand the things of heaven; if we no longer do understand them, it is because we have closed our eyes and ears, for centuries perhaps, or because it might have bothered us to listen and look.

Listen and look then! The light can come to you in the simplest, most unexpected way. It can speak through the mouth of a poor itinerant or of a man of genius—everything is worthy of our attention. He who at this moment hears but does not listen, does he know whether next year, or next century, he might not be seeking anxiously to receive what he is neglecting today? We must fight against our likes and dislikes of the moment, and take what life brings us—it is always better than what we crave. Seen from the point of view of the Absolute, things, beings, events, ideas, creations, collectives, and all forms of universal existence appear in their true identity only in the core or central plane of the earth—in its heart, and in our heart. Their true stature is then refracted in various ways on all other planes. For example, taking a walk gives pleasure to the body; for the restaurant along the way it means a financial gain; for the trodden-down grass it is a calamity. A trial, on the other hand, is the clearing of a field of brambles. An epidemic here below is only a harvest elsewhere. All our joys are made of the pain of others. True knowledge, then, is what shows us, behind this or that refraction, the living

THE HEALINGS OF CHRIST

spirit of the thing; it depends on the purity of our inner vision, our moral refinement, and the favor of the Holy Spirit.

The current social and international situation is the result of the same drive towards free individualism that gave rise to the Reformation, Freemasonry, the French Revolution, the political events of 1789 and 1848, the *Internationale*, and the French Republic. But this impulse, so noble, so generous, was driven—by reaction against traditionalist Catholicism—to admit only reason and to replace the cult of God with the cult of Humanity. On the other hand, history teaches us that the principle of authority, in politics as in religion, tends also to excesses. These struggles, these balancings-out of hostile doctrines, are in the very nature of earthly matters. In nature, there are no circles or spheres—all is ellipse or ovoid. Because God over and above nature intervenes in nature there are no closed curves or solids: there are only parabolas, or should I rather say, paraboloids.

That is why the Word makes use of parables.[3]

This is no mere word-play. Assuredly, the name Rambouillet does not come from the root-word Ram, any more than the word crystal comes from Christ. Nor are all red vegetables equally beneficial for the blood! But in analogies, homonyms, and homophones, there is nonetheless sometimes a glimmer. There is light everywhere; but down here, everything is so very complicated. Earthly forms, seen from above are the outcomes of innumerable forces. If an oak leaf is one shade of green and a willow leaf another, there may be two or three thousand causes for this difference; and their virtues also differ. Then again, color is not the

---

[3] The French *parabole* can mean both parabola and parable.

The Kingdom of Heaven

only signifier; there are others: shape, context, veining, flavor, smell, density. However that may be, the fact that these two leaf species are green indicates that they share a common property, just one.

And so, when the evangelist writes that Jesus spoke in parables, we must first note that these parables are not to be taken as examples, similitudes, comparisons, symbolisms, allegories, or any sort of rhetoric. Moreover, one must accept that between the reader and Jesus there is a great distance, a vast space that is not a desert but a world—in fact, several worlds—peopled with lights, substances, forces, inhabitants, all of which may deflect the visual ray and deform the sound of his divine voice.

One must also know that, as soon as the auditor has done what is necessary, Jesus abolishes the distance. He even diminishes it to the degree that we submit to his kind law. Intuitive insights do not go very far. It is no small task to make our intuitions so pure, so spiritual, so vigorous, that they can wait upon the truth itself where it stands, i.e., at the center of ourselves where the sparkle of the Word shines. Had the romantics and monists, had Bergson, William James, and our young surrealists, understood that there is the Created and the Uncreated, they would not have made of man an omniscient god. They would not imagine that the pinnacle of art or of thought is to place oneself in a receptive state, waiting and taking note of images as they pass by. Doubtless, the true mystic stands before God in a receptive state; but, first of all, he works constantly at rendering all his physical and soul organs capable of receiving God. Now, the adept of the East follows this discipline according to a system of traditional science. In this undertaking, however, he is mistaken, since any system of knowledge is provisional. The servant of Christ, on the other hand, who forgets his own perfecting so as to think only of obedience to his work, who permits Christ to act in his stead, does not err, and will reach the goal.

If, then, the *spoken* lessons of the incarnate Word are parables, the *actions* of the eternal Word are parables also. The Word broadcasts creatures into the fields of the universe, and just as the seed sown in winter goes to seed again the following autumn, so we find ourselves at the end of the cosmic year to be the same seeds we were at the beginning, except that we have multiplied and grown. With this difference, however: that if the seed of the harvest is identical in type to the seed of the sowing (and here, too, a great deal could be said, because life keeps ascending), if for us the ellipse in matter is about to close upon itself—the sacrifice of the Word opens this ellipse, sending its second focus to infinity and thereby transforming it into a parabola or parable.

If men as unknowing bearers (as they so often are) of a word from the Word are often sad, worried, or lost, if they see badly or do not see at all, it is because they have not accepted the divine word that the Word whispered in them—because they don't want it. At first they fear it. Then rebel against it. Later on they will accept it, but alas, after how many battles! They could be happy right away, but matter, the world, and reason fascinate them.

We are an ellipse; the adept tries to become a circle, uniting the ellipse's twin foci into one. Christ teaches, however, that we must open the ellipse by projecting one of the foci to infinity. Closed curves in fact are "destiny"; open curves are "freedom." Do not the countenances around us, with their taut, embittered mouths and withered, calculating

The Kingdom of Heaven

eyes, tell of an angry struggle against destiny? Men deny it: they proclaim themselves free; they reject any heritage whatsoever; they want nothing more to do with law or hierarchy. But you can only rebel against your tyrant. And so they feel like prisoners who won't admit that their rebellions only tighten their shackles another notch. There are a great many intelligent and superior minds today. They have read, analyzed, admired, understood everything that is human. They have acquired a surfeit of culture. Their brain suffers indigestion, their nerves are on edge. That is why artists and poets with refined temperaments try to recapture some freshness and appetite by returning to primitive art forms, to the stammerings of antique lyricism. But they only manage to concoct an artificial naiveté. Spontaneous enthusiasm cannot be simulated. Man, by himself, cannot return to the candor of the child. For that, he must accept the help of the great Healer of souls. But he does not want it. Let us wait, then—for no rebellion wearies the patience of God.

Moreover, a word carries farther than the one who utters it. The thoughts preceding it may someday soon be re-echoed in the proclamations of a new school. Our discourses follow their own little parabola. And I repeat: the stories Jesus told his disciples were not allegories. When he explains them, he does not comment on them, as did the ancient initiators. Jesus is not an ordinary storyteller. When Jesus speaks, he creates the thing of which he speaks. When he speaks of seeds sown in different soils, or speaks of trees, of leavening, of pearls, he does not "employ" an image—it is of himself he speaks. The sowings are himself, as also is the seed. The spoonful of leavening is himself. This pearl is himself. In a certain secret place, the pearl, the seed, the leaven, live. These things are already in the eternal kingdom. At the very moment Jesus names them, they are descending into the soul of the earth and begin to exist there. What most men refuse to understand is that the pearl beyond price lies within their reach. As for the miraculous leavening, they have but to take it. And it is up to them to receive and nourish the seeds of light where truth, beauty, and eternal goodness lie dormant. Because of the all-powerful word of the Word, these facts, these phenomena, these objects, are located in the center of our world, whence they radiate. When their radiation falls upon a stone or plant or animal of our globe, a new body, new plant, new animal is produced. When this radiation falls upon a man's spirit and is refracted thence upon his intellect, feeling, and body, a more beautiful form of art, a better form of strength, a truer idea, is engendered. All of this, along with many other collateral consequences, is the slow descent of the kingdom of God, the progressive realization of God's will.

The Parable of the Sower

AT FIRST SIGHT, the parable of the sower seems open to numerous interpretations. One could easily imagine that there are other sowers besides the Word; that elementals, gods, and angels also sow seeds into the human person; that the living forms of the physical world seed our sensorium, just as passionate feelings and artistic emotions fertilize our sensibility, and concepts germinate in our intelligence. We could also imagine that in relation to each other we are in turn sowers, seeds, and soil. Such hypotheses do not correspond to truth, and I only enumerate them as examples of

The Kingdom of Heaven

the distance separating practical, realistic understandings of the gospel lessons from the symbolisms by which these lessons have been rendered insipid. Such attempts are likely to multiply in this century, where the self-assurance of innovators trumpet proudly age-old truths they do not understand.

The essence of a seed is that it carries within it both the dynamic totality of the creature from which it springs and the power to reproduce one or more copies thereof when placed in a suitable environment. The stone possesses its seminal virtue, just like the plant, the beast, man, and the aborigine of the invisible world. But this virtue stops at the reproduction of the physical form. No matter what our physiologists claim, parents do not transmit the essentials of their temperament or mentality to their progeny. On the contrary, the self, for whom the hour has come to work down-here by means of certain moral and intellectual forces, is directed to the parents whose physiological and psychological faculties will furnish it with the most favorable environment for the experiences its intended destiny imposes upon it. Beings, things, events, and environments do not create in us; they imprint images on us—they solicit us or push us aside, they suggest to us, they sometimes tyrannize us; but they cannot bring out of us a new being, any more than we can truly create. All we can do is copy.

Also, there is only one sower in the fields of the universe: it is the Word, Jesus Christ. He alone sows life, because he alone is life. It is not life that we give our children; we give them existence only; in fact, we do not even give them that, we only pass it on to them. If we want to be born into life, we must understand, we must feel, we must see, that we do not live, that nothing in us really lives, that we move in a world of shadows, that we are entranced by ghosts that we think of in images. And, at the same time, we must respect these shadows, cherish these ghosts, seize these images, because in them lie, like the seed in the dust of the road, the marvelous possibilities of our birth in God.

These conclusions, let me repeat once again, apply as much to the individual as to the nation: in the individual, they apply to every form of activity, to every social position; in the nation, they apply to every organization, every enterprise, every attitude towards other nations.

The Word is the only authentic sower. All of us, races peoples, and individuals, bodies, souls, or spirits, are the sole terrain, because man alone has the privilege of being able to communicate immediately with God; all other creatures—except angels—receive eternal light through man. It is therefore of the utmost importance to learn how to receive the seeds of eternity. How can we be neither the hard ground of the road, nor the stones, nor the brambles? Jesus tells us: "you must have a pure and good heart, and fulfill the divine commandments with perseverance."

You are experienced enough to understand the depth and to feel the richness of these simple words, but you often have to deal with people who like complications. Here are a few topics you may use for discussions with such people.

Let us consider, for example, the work of the human mind in general.

This work consists of research and inquiries regarding the world: about facts, ideas, and methods for individual development, as well as about our social, moral and intellectual constructions. There are two ways of conducting these inquiries. The first way is that of the sentimental, the intuitive, the emotive (passionate), the free thinkers; in various ways this is romanticism as represented by Montaigne,

The Kingdom of Heaven

Rousseau, Delacroix, Proudhon, and Bergson. The second way is that of the systematists, the traditionalists, the partisans of authority; this is classicism and Catholic theology as expressed by Bossuet, Ingres, Auguste Comte, and Charles Maurras. The first way is that of the Eastern genius; the second is that of the Greco-Latin genius. Perfection lies in a synthesis of the two ways; but such a synthesis is rare and does not last. Gustave Flaubert calls attention to it in his dialogue between the Sphinx and the Chimera. Dante, da Vinci, and Racine attained it at times in their particular fields. But on the common, universal path, Christ is its unequalled model, and the gospel the perfect method.

Our contemporaries have an exasperated horror of rules; they don't want to obey any rule that they themselves have not dictated. In overlooking man's long-standing impotence in fulfilling his desires, they fail to see that it is in obedience that he can find the most solid happiness and the most lasting strength. Faced with perpetual disillusionment, the proud become pessimistic, like Chateaubriand; but the humble turn to heaven, humble themselves to the core, and soon receive the whole sum of certainty and peace that is compatible with human nature. It is the great lesson of Jesus to achieve perfect harmony by remaining simple and natural. But most misunderstand this. Depending on their character, some take the authoritarian part, others the libertarian path. Now, an excess of authority breeds revolutions, and an excess of liberty raises up tyrannies.

But, let us not stray from our parable. The divine seed, life, true intelligence, healthy feeling, volitional energy—they all fall on the path, on the stones, among the brambles, or into good earth.

The good earth is that organic harmony resulting from

THE HEALINGS OF CHRIST

the normal combination of all elements: dust on the path, a few stones, the detritus of wild shrubs where the seed finds its needed nourishment. We might say the brambles are the disordered vegetation of the libertarian tendency, the stones are the arid nakedness of the authoritarian tendency that in the end undoes itself, and the dust on the path is the amorphous, the anarchic, the inconsistent, which is where the excesses of one or the other system inevitably end.

From dust we come, to dust we return—and not only with regard to our bodies. Whether a citizen, a worker, a thinker, an artist, or a religious—all begin by struggling in the dust, and everyone must make a choice. The quality of this choice is extremely important. Will we choose to submit to one rule or to another? Will we choose pride in order to call ourselves liberated? The answer depends on rank or classification either in the army of the Antichrist or in the phalanx of Christ. It is not merely a matter of enlisting. We have to *do* something. The profession of soldier must be *fulfilled*. We must become good at chores and good at battle. We must learn to freely obey. The synthesis of opposites is everywhere: the Word, the "prime mover," the only perfect One, sows himself on earth, in the inert, in the "unmoved."

Catholicism also is twofold: it is the interior Christianity of each believer, and the exterior Church—a monument of indestructible stone, both in the social order and in the intellectual order. Look at Israel, the people once the most authoritarian in religion and politics, that in the wake of its diasporas and persecutions has become the most active of revolutionary ferments. Of course I am speaking somewhat broadly, or crudely here, neglecting nuances and transitions that would require volumes to expound. I am only setting

The Kingdom of Heaven

signposts as an aid to classify our studies. Our subject is infinitely complex, and whatever may be the terrain we explore, signposts are useful—even if they may not give precise measures. Having said this, let us resume.

In any effort where God is not the object, let us beware of extremes. Let us never entirely trust our intelligence or our will. Rather, let us trust our heart, to the extent we purify its impulses by an inflexible discipline over its selfishness and our laziness. The Council of Trent established that attrition (i.e., repentance brought about by fear of hell) is not sufficient to assure our salvation, but that there must also be contrition, that is, regret for having offended God. And this view is that of common sense.

Carrying this remark to the collective level of societies, we will understand that all ways of being are useful to the life of a race. It too needs a discipline like that of Rome, a freedom like that of the Reformation, even (at certain moments) excessive individualism, like that into which precipitate the Jews of today. But, above all, the life of a race needs love, this silent love that dust, stones, or brambles deny to life, but that good arable soil offers without further ado—that gives itself entirely to the seed (whereas the others hold something back, respecting themselves alone).

Thus the self-willed, the libertarian, the inert will all of them fail; those alone, people or race, will triumph who know how to receive and then organize; who will have known how to be passive, then active; Ionian, then Dorian; passionate, then deliberate; tyrant of his selfishness, then fraternal to selfishness (or rather, to the sufferings of others); hard for himself, then finally tender for others.

THE HEALINGS OF CHRIST

⊕

Let us not forget, however, that every favor carries a responsibility. The clod of earth where the grain falls does not remain inert; it works, it strives as much as the grain; let us imitate it. What the great Sower entrusts to us asks for all our concern; it must be implemented on every occasion—simply, humbly, discreetly, but constantly.

The tiny little seed that was sown in you is asked to grow; your numerous requests will pull it upwards, as the air and the sun draw the stem out of the ground; your disciplines and your pains will nourish it, as humus nourishes the bud from below.

I therefore ask you for a patient and careful cultivation of the seed received; a free, easy, confident, cheerful preparation to receive other precious seeds. For this great Sower, whom we claim to serve—no one imagines what trouble He goes through to come down here to bring the brilliant seed of light into our dark hearts; to reduce the formidable stars of the Infinite to the miserable capacity of our crippled courage; to weaken the dazzling flashes of the unrevealed heavens, so that by touching us and this poor globe that carries us, we are not instantly reduced to ashes. Our rigorous duty is to put all our strength into recognizing the immense labor of him who, alone in the world, loves us in truth.

The times we live in are most depressing; the situation of our homeland is most uncertain; it resembles the worst situations on our front lines during the war; everyone is anxious; we cannot help but feel the general concern. And yet we must not give in to it.

This concern seems deeper today than it seems to have been at other equally critical epochs in our history. This is

The Kingdom of Heaven

because in the past, social foundations did not appear solid, since they were in the process of being built, whereas today, when we feel them moving, we fear it is from old age. Also, our characters are much less strong, less well-tempered. Too many reject tradition, too many no longer want authority or divine hope; too many no longer want simple reason. We cannot do anything about it. We were born in this time. We need not moan about it; we just have to face the situation squarely.

Whenever you are weary, turn your eyes to the constancy of our Father, to the incomprehensible perseverance of his Son. I am not referring to what he has done for the universe since the first moment of time—that perspective would be too vast. Look at what he has done for our earth and for humankind over the last twenty centuries. He represents himself in the figure of the great Sower, but the sowing he practices is not the easier sort of our farmers because he is both the Sower and the Seed. The farmer casts his handfuls of seed into the furrows, then relies on the good soil, sun, and rain; but the Word does not cast the seeds of light from out of heaven; he takes pains first to pass through the zodiacs before coming here-below. This journey lasts for centuries, as you know, and each of the steps of the Eternal Pilgrim is an incarnation on the star where he sets his foot. Imagine all this signifies of sufferings, anguish, crucifixions, and infinite hopes constantly disappointed. Remember that since his ascension, Christ has never ceased watching over our world, that he sees only rubble and brambles where not a single sheaf of corn springs up. Consider that he has perhaps at times taken on a body secretly in order to prevent this globe from rolling into nothingness. Consider that from among the billions of human beings who have lived throughout the world's historical existence, there are perhaps no more than some few hundreds of these sheaves that have reached perfect maturity. Undoubtedly, generations are not constantly renewed—the same ones come back repeatedly; but despite all this, to our impatience the results of divine patience seem meager.

Remember that you are each, like Christ, at the head of a world: we ourselves are our field; we are the sowers of ourselves; and, if our person is tiny, compared to a star, the grains that we must help to germinate there are also small and of low vitality. Let us not be discouraged. Is Jesus discouraged? Has he not proportioned our work to our strength? Does not the soldier feel his courage increase in measure as the battle becomes the more critical? And do we not know that victory is ours?

Forgive me if I tell you things that do not satisfy you; but, since sometimes you confide in me your troubles, your disappointments, your successes too, without saying anything about this profound joy in which the soldier of heaven lives, I think you do not possess this joy. And, as I know that Christ gives it without fail to anyone who serves him without respite, I conclude that there must still be dull moments in you. But this should not be. You can make the ineffable peace of heaven surround you.

⊕

We owe everything to heaven and do nothing for it. If it were possible for us to see the innumerable gifts that the Father constantly distributes to us, and the imperceptible requitals that our poor virtues are, we would be terrified and would despair. An ocean is given us, but we sprinkle only a few drops of water upon the arid soil of our field.

The Kingdom of Heaven

Fortunately, we do not measure the frightful disproportion. Everywhere in nature there are sandy paths, stones, brambles—and only a quarter thereof is good soil; but these sandy paths, rocks, and brambles depend upon man to improve them. Man is the king of creation, alas! because he only wants to be king to pressure his subjects, whereas he should distribute to them all his wealth. Our self-importance crushes us before Justice, and we do not even recognize the inexhaustible Mercy.

We should constantly be attentive to the possibility of receiving a seed from the great Sower. Contrary to what the sages believe, creation is not finished. It goes on, and each earthly minute, place, or organ can be the point of arrival of a particle of divine life.

Since our heart is still too weak to be in two places at once, we should use each free moment to reposition ourselves before God. We should do so without reservation or anxiety, but quietly and with tranquility, without rapture, yet without ever feeling dejection.

First and foremost, we should never allow ourselves to be distracted from God. Next, we must ensure that trials do not turn us away from him. Our heart is stone covered with a thin layer of soil. To disintegrate it, crumble it, and slowly turn it into arable ground, we need snow, rain, sun, the lightning of the storm, and also the pickaxe of certain laborers—by which I mean the various sufferings we accept so badly: poverty, slander, mourning, and disappointments. We must also not let grow within us longings for earthly happiness that, seen in the light, are only brambles. Finally, as Jesus expressly says, our heart must become completely honest (doing no harm any creature) and completely good (doing good to every creature).

THE HEALINGS OF CHRIST

Note here that all psychic and mental states are, in reality, living beings. Vices, defects, virtues, tendencies pre-exist before and after their manifestation in us, in plant, animal, and pseudo-human forms. So it is that for moralists and philosophers parables are allegories, but for those whose eyes the Spirit has opened they are exact descriptions.

Let us take care to resist all temporal influences; let us only accept the eternal ones; let us look first to Christ.

Parables of the Grain

THE DUTY of the one who has received is to transmit in turn: whether it be an intellectual light, a force of compassion, wealth, a therapeutic power—it must be shared with everyone, completely. One of the effects of the messianic work is to bring to the fore what was unknown until then, to shed light on the inhabitants of the caves, to render the mysteries comprehensible. Let us be secret only about what can serve evil—and about our neighbors' faults.

Every man receives, with existence, a spark of divine light with life. But he who does not profit by that spark, who does not give it fuel, can see it taken away and conferred on brothers who have taken good care of the spark they already possess. When we hear or see something of God, let us hold on to it with appreciation, with humility; let us put it into practice. From the proud will be taken even what they believe to be theirs.

It is not that our work has a direct impact on the growth of the spiritual seeds within us; it only improves the quality of the soil and chases away the clouds interfering with the rays of the mystical sun. Thus, the grain of wheat once sown, the ground once fertilized, the stalk of corn keeps on

The Kingdom of Heaven

growing without the farmer knowing how it grows. We need only perform our duty as best we can; heaven takes care of the rest.

It is not only heaven that sows the fields of our spirit with seed. The Adversary has received this power also. In the great majority of cases, weeds choke the wheat, but it also happens that the wheat improves the weeds. Even in the domain of our freedom, good or bad actions are also seeds—which is why we often reap disgust, sadness, apathy.

Good and evil are everywhere side by side, and the angels of the Lord let them grow together for fear of destroying a little good by weeding too early, while the crop is still young. It is only at the coming of the great Judge that the bad are thrown into the fire of suffering, while the good increase the divine treasure by establishing in the very place in the world where they evolved a colony of the Kingdom.

As for hell, it is indeed eternal, in the sense that, from the beginning to the end of a creation, there are always places where we suffer; but no one remains forever under the rule of demons. The angelic harvesters let nothing go to waste, but neither do destroy anything. We ourselves are in a field where the master has sown wheat; and at night, when the gendarmes have their backs turned, the sorcerer comes to sow weeds there. The soil is duty-bound, first of all, to nourish the wheat. If it does not do this, know that the master will turn it over before it is entrusted with a new sowing.

Final Parables

"THERE ARE no real fruits for man except those that grow from his own ground," says Lodoik, Count of Divonne. Heaven gives us the seed. For it to grow, time and effort are

THE HEALINGS OF CHRIST

needed—because in nature everything is subject to the law of time, and nothing is independent of it. A psychic faculty needs a basis, a soil in which to take root. If, for example, goodness grows in us, its exercise implies prudence, tact, ingenuity, mental qualities, muscular strength, self-control. Without these we would lack the energy needed for acts of charity, and virtue would wither away in us.

As we go about our daily work, we can only look forward with confidence to the results of mystical cultivation. The former may seem insignificant in the eyes of reason; but be assured that heaven will take care of the latter.

Just as a little leaven is sufficient to raise three measures of flour, so the light acts on our spirit as well as on our vitality and our body; but its operation is so subtle that we hardly ever feel it. Light thus penetrates all the planes of the world, although it is hidden. This is what theologians have partially understood when they explain that the woman of the gospel is the Church, which conceals in its three great human families the leaven of its doctrine (Dom Gueranger).

These teachings, which to those who can hear them seem so simple, were not known to the sages of old. They had little idea of the divine Presence, active and real; they conceived of it as a river of fluid force, like a breath descending from the high peaks of the world, whose glorious inhabitants from time to time sent to the children of the earth a vivifying influx. But the path that leads to the Absolute was not yet traced in their time. In the drama of the cosmos they could perceive only the balanced play of natural interchanges.

In the course of his daily labor, the farmer finds, without searching for it, the celestial treasure. The merchant searches, but finds only a pearl, even if it be of great price.

The Kingdom of Heaven

The Kingdom is closer at hand for the meek. In fact, as soon as Jesus has made his presence felt in us, all other things leave us indifferent: we abandon friendships, loves, riches, sciences, renown; all the places these passing guests occupied in the apartments of our mind and spirit are now free: all the strength they drew upon now goes to the service of the Master; all worries vanish; all desires become unified; all ignorance is illuminated by the victorious flame of love.

⊕

The parable of the fishes is analogous to that of the wheat and the tares.

This series of similitudes traces all the modes of divine solicitude: the distribution of light, its culture, its growth, the struggle of meekness against evil, the all-powerful propagation of the Spirit, his mystery, the beatitude he dispenses, and finally the classification of the disciples. Moreover, those who have worn their chains and even so have helped others wear theirs, are admitted to total freedom.

When his children have behaved, the father, in the evening, empties the treasure boxes where he stores the precious objects he has collected. Little by little he shows them to the children and instructs them, while making it a game. The curiosity of children awakens their taste, sharpens their intelligence, sometimes even indicates to them their vocation. Likewise, Christ came to make us admire some of the splendors of his Kingdom, so that the desire arises in us to see them all one day, and to use them, according to what Christ promised in the name of his Father.

But there are many other wonders than those described in the gospel. The time will surely come when we will be able to contemplate them all in the house of God. To get there, we must not seek the reward directly, for the understanding we can ourselves acquire of the mysteries can never be more than partial. The burden would be too heavy for our shoulders—we would develop a swelled head on our puny body. We must do our duty. When we have completed it, the Father will give us the inheritance, because, as for ourselves, our ego, in both its conscious and unconscious parts, is composed of nothing but natural forces, which can only feed on natural, i.e., *relative*, nourishment. The resulting sciences and powers are thus bound to be incomplete and full of error. Pure Spirit alone is *absolute* truth, because it is unfettered by time or space.

Wait, then, for the baptism of the Spirit, and you will know all, and all will be submitted to you.

www.ingramcontent.com/pod-product-compliance
Lightning Source LLC
Chambersburg PA
CBHW020326170426
43200CB00006B/289